P9-EMR-650

CRAFTING the CUSTOMER EXPERIENCE FOR PEOPLE NOT LIKE* YOU

How to DELIGHT AND ENGAGE THE CUSTOMERS YOUR COMPETITORS DON'T UNDERSTAND

KELLY McDONALD

John Wiley & Sons, Inc.

Cover design: Gearbox

Published by John Wiley & Sons, Inc., Hoboken, New Jersey.
Published simultaneously in Canada.

For general information on our other products and services or for technical support, please contact our Customer Care Department within the United States at (800) 762-2974, outside the United States at (317) 572-3993 or fax (317) 572-4002.

Wiley publishes in a variety of print and electronic formats and by print-on-demand. Some material included with standard print versions of this book may not be included in e-books or in print-on-demand. If this book refers to media such as a CD or DVD that is not included in the version you purchased, you may download this material at http://booksupport.wiley.com. For more information about Wiley products, visit www.wiley.com.

ISBN 978-1-118-36072-9 (cloth); ISBN 978-1-118-46164-8 (ebk); ISBN 978-1-118-46166-2 (ebk); ISBN 978-1-118-46167-9 (ebk)

Printed in the United States of America

10 9 8 7 6 5 4

To my Powers,
my air,
my light,
my refuge,
and my momentum

Contents

Acknowledgments

The words *thank you* don't seem adequate when it comes to acknowledging the people who helped me with this book. Whether it was for their contributions, their wisdom, their insight, their support, or their patience, I relied on all of them for months on end.

To my editor, Richard Narramore, for his steady guidance and skill. You always know just what to say to keep me on track. And you cheered me on when I was flagging. It meant the world to me. Thank you.

To Lydia Dimitriadis, Christine Moore, and the entire team at John Wiley & Sons who make a manuscript turn into a book. I so appreciate your talent, coaching, dedication, and hard work.

To John, for hanging in there and doing this with me again. Thanks for all your help and the hundreds of hours of research in finding the best examples—good and bad—of the customer experience.

To Jennifer Martin, my BFF forever, for understanding and supporting me, always. And for letting me go underground for months at a time, only to pick up right where we left off. Love you and need you in my life, even when I don't tell you that.

To Adam Fitzgerald, for always, always saving the day, and inevitably, at the most inconvenient times. And specifically, for recovering Chapter 2 after I inadvertently saved over it. Thanks also for having the coolest dog in the world, Turbo.

To my inner circle, for letting me be me. And for being right there for me when I finally came to the surface: Robert Swafford, Katie Hollar, Lynne Swihart, Jerry Martinez, Cliff Bohaker, Adam Bowden, Melissa Timmerman, Tina Harrison, Todd Young, William Siskron, Joel Benjamin Griffin, Alejandro Gonzalez, Tayfun Aşut, Gregorio Kishketon, Trace Symonds, Alejandro Perez, Matthew Skelly, Shawn Quish, Luis Rodriguez, Darin Iglehart, Anthony Derego, Andrea Cleverley Howard, Randy McCauley, and Ronnie Sullivan. I count on you for fun, but you have all become so much more than that.

To Jessica Levin, for providing outstanding expertise and insights and helping with, possibly, the most important chapter. Respect, girl, respect.

To Cliff Bohaker, for your ability to make the most mundane errand an adventure and a blast and for being a wonderful friend. Oh, and your cupcakes rock.

To Pam Atherton, who knows how to give a damn good pep talk and an even better interview. And for knowing exactly when a girl needs some new, expensive makeup.

To Kenja Purkey, for the ability to make me laugh, always. And for taking the wheel on the work I simply could not do while writing this book. Your talent and your brain leave me in awe.

To Katie Hollar, "Black Swan," for sending me texts that were either supportive or snarky and for somehow always knowing which I needed at that exact moment.

To Melinda Fishman, for helping out with stories and examples and understanding the hiatus that writing imposed on our daily telephone chats.

To Melissa Timmerman, for sending me a text every few weeks that said, "You alive? Just checking." It always touched me and made me smile. Thank you.

To all those who contributed and helped with specific insights and anecdotes:

Breanna Ridge (you have the world's greatest smile and attitude), Kim Edwards (I always turn to you for customer insights—you are the best), Daniel Eaton (aka "Pookie" forever), Chandra Livingston (for making time to help out a complete stranger), and Joe Martin and Jake Martin, my "other family" and my dear friends forever.

And to my clients, who have cheered me on, encouraged me, and put in advance orders for the book.

CHAPTER 1
How Tweaking the Customer Experience Grows Your Business

You didn't pick up this book because you want to know how to provide terrific customer service. There are plenty of good books and articles on the subject, and they all cover the basic principles of being polite, efficient, and responsive to customers' needs. You picked up this book because you're smart enough to know that the *business climate out there is changing*. In fact, it's already changed. It's not easy to provide a level of customer service that resonates with all your customers anymore. It's more fragmented than that. People are not "one size fits all," and therefore, one sweeping customer service approach isn't going to cut it when it comes to satisfying—much less *delighting*—a diverse group of customers.

Providing a great experience to different kinds of people isn't just the right thing to do. It's the *strategic* thing to do. Crafting a customer experience that caters to people not like you will improve your business in five ways:

1. It will grow your business by bringing in *new customers*.
2. It will give you a *significant competitive edge*, since your competition is probably either ignoring diverse customer groups or, at best, underserving them.
3. It will *increase customer loyalty* and therefore *customer retention*.
4. It will help *differentiate* you from other businesses or similar enterprises.
5. It will give you a *greater understanding of different customer groups*, providing key insights into what people who are not like you want and what they respond to, which will generate even more creative ideas and unique ways to delight customers.

Any one of these five ways is reason enough to be reading this book. Business nowadays is tough and fiercely competitive, and no one can afford to overlook a customer group. But when you combine all five of these ways to deliver an exceptional customer experience to people not like you, they add up to a truly unbeatable market position.

It doesn't matter what business you're in or what level you're at in an organization; if you work, you have customers. Even if you work internally at a company and don't interact with any of the company's customers directly, trust me—you still have customers. If you're an administrative assistant, your customer may be the team you work with. If you're in accounting, your customer is the entire company, because that's who benefits from sound accounting skills. If you work in a small office, your customer may be your boss. And if you work with clients or customers directly, then of course, you must deliver great customer service to keep them happy and retain them as customers.

We *ALL* have customers. If you work, you have customers.

This book will help you find creative ways to develop loyal customers by crafting specific experiences for major customer segments such as women, Latinos, African Americans, and different age/generational groups. Chances are, your competitors aren't paying attention to these groups, or not as much attention as they should be. If you can find an overlooked group and delight almost every member of that group, then you've found the next growth strategy for your business.

Providing a good customer experience is a pretty basic business concept, right? But that's not what this book is about. It's about how you can deliver an exceptional experience to *people* who are ***not like you***. This can be difficult, because often our differences are subtle. That's why your competitors aren't developing customer service strategies for diverse markets: they don't see an obvious "hole" in the market for that. They simply don't recognize the need to do it. And that's precisely where your opportunity lies: by creating a customer experience that addresses a specific customer group's needs and wants, you can differentiate yourself from your competition and grow your business with new, incremental customers.

To figure out how to best serve someone not like you, you need insight. You need to address areas such as hiring and training. And you need to expand your thinking to encompass the *entire experience:* what happens to or with a customer before, during, and after purchasing your product or service. Let me give you an example:

When you get a chip or crack in your automobile's windshield, you call an auto glass/windshield repair company. Almost all of these companies will come to your home or office to do the repair on-site. This provides a tremendous benefit to the customer, because it allows that person to keep doing what he or she needs and wants to do (working, for example) and saves that person time by eliminating the need to go anywhere. And it's also practical; many times, the windshield may be so damaged that it's not safe to drive the vehicle because the driver's visibility is impaired. Coming to your home or place of business is a wonderful *service* aspect of the product that these companies sell. Their *product* is auto glass repair, but they provide a valuable customer *service* by coming to you.

DIFFERENT CUSTOMERS CARE ABOUT DIFFERENT THINGS

Not all customers are the same. We don't all have the same priorities, concerns, or needs. Many women, for example, are uncomfortable having strangers come to their homes, particularly if that stranger is a man. I have several single female friends who *always* choose to meet vendors and repairmen at their offices or workplaces whenever possible, because they don't want a stranger to know that they live alone. But it's not always realistic to meet someone at your place of work. After all, if you need a plumber to fix your toilet, that plumber must come to your home.

Safelite Auto Glass crafted a customer service benefit that was clearly *developed for women.* Once an appointment is scheduled, they informally "introduce" the technician to the customer by e-mail and include a photo of the technician who will be doing the work; they also inform the customer what time the technician will arrive. Wow! Although this is a service that everyone can benefit from, it's clearly designed to put women's minds at ease. By knowing what the technician looks like and what time to expect him or her, clients' anxiety of having a "stranger" come to their homes is reduced. What a terrific service! It's so simple—but it shows how the company really understands women and is working hard to be a woman's preferred provider of auto glass repair. They are providing a solution to a specific fear or anxiety that many women have: having a stranger come to their home. You know what else I like about this example? It costs so little but means so much. E-mailing a photo of the tech is a low-cost or no-cost step, but it gives the customer *priceless peace of mind*. It also tells that female customer that she is seen, appreciated, valued, and understood—and isn't that what we all want?

Every customer wants to feel special and important; we want the places we spend our money to welcome, appreciate, respect, and value us. But the customer experience needs to be more than that in today's business climate; it must also be more nuanced, refined, and unique—to move from "mass" to "targeted." This doesn't mean that each and every customer needs to have a customized experience. It means that brands must make their services more targeted and tailored to specific customer *groups*. You can provide various types of customer service—or service in different *ways*—to diverse groups of people. By doing so, you let that customer group know that you recognize them and their specific needs, wants, hopes, or fears. You show that you are responding to those with specialized service offerings that are right for them. And those customers and prospects will feel so valued that they'll reward you with even more of their business.

This book will show you how to create customer service experiences that are right for people *not like you*—and will show that you don't have to break the bank to do it. You'll learn how to design distinctive types of experiences that will surprise and delight your customers and prospects and keep them coming back to you for more. It's a proven fact that customer retention is far less costly than acquiring new customers. So why not focus on giving each and every customer an experience that delights them, engages them, and exceeds their expectations? Doing so will turn those happy customers into your greatest advocates. They become ambassadors for your brand, product, or service, spreading referrals and goodwill about you to their networks of family, friends, and associates. Why wouldn't you want to put that no-cost power to work for you? Why wouldn't you want to give diverse groups the customer service *they* want and need?

WHY I DISLIKE THE "D" WORD

This is a good place for me to define what I mean by "diverse" customers. I'm not a big fan of the word *diversity* these days, for two reasons: First, I think many people have what I call diversity fatigue. They're tired of hearing about how important diversity is. They've heard the "diversity lecture" at work for years now and are burned out on it. They see or hear the word and automatically tune out. It's not that they don't respect different cultures, races, ethnicities, and norms; it's just that there has been so much focus on diversity that people are tired of the subject, even though it's an important one.

The second reason I tend to shy away from using the word *diversity* is that, in my experience, most people automatically default to thinking of diversity in terms of racial and ethnic differences. And although that's very important and we'll tackle customer service for some key racial and ethnic groups in this book, I don't think that even begins to cover the breadth of meaning of the word *diversity.*

THE DEFINITION OF "PEOPLE NOT LIKE YOU"

I define *diversity* as "any way that I can be different from you." For example, if you have kids and I don't, we're likely to have different priorities and face different pressures. Your entire focus shifts when you become a parent, because it has to. Parents think about and evaluate everything differently from people who aren't parents. But that difference has nothing to do with race, ethnicity, age, or even gender; it simply has to do with whether or not you have children.

Someone who lives in a major metropolitan area is different from someone who lives in a small, rural community. Imagine the customer service implications of each scenario. The city dweller may appreciate speed and efficiency above all else. Super busy and rushed all the time, the city dweller has to spend valuable time fighting traffic just to get where he or she wants to go and has to fight crowds everywhere. If you were a merchant catering to this customer, perhaps the greatest customer service experience you could provide would be one that *saves time and reduces hassles.*

But the rural customer may have none of those same issues. He or she may enjoy, above all else, the friendly, personal interaction received from someone considered to be a *neighbor.* A rural customer may perceive a merchant who provides a fast, efficient, no-nonsense experience as uncaring or aloof. On the other hand, that person will see a merchant who greets the customer by name, asks about his or her family, and spends time chatting about the local weather or football game as friendly, a local fixture, and someone who can be depended on. The merchant makes it clear that he or she isn't too busy to spend a few minutes talking. In this example, *diversity* can encompass lifestyle and *how* people want to be serviced. Again, this example has nothing to do with race or ethnicity; it has to do with the attributes of city living versus rural living.

Of course, you already know all this. You picked up this book because the title promised you'd learn about providing customer service to people *not* like you. Whoever you are, wherever you live, and even *however* you live, there are lots of people who are very different from you. As a businessperson and a professional, you know that the time has come to figure out how to cater to all of your customers'—and potential customers'—needs and desires. Although marketing will bring customers to your door, it can't guarantee that they'll buy anything. You make the sale when a customer *experiences* what you have to offer.

NOT CUSTOMER SERVICE, BUT CUSTOMER *EXPERIENCE*

Make no mistake; the customer experience doesn't simply entail what customers go through when they buy something. It also encompasses what happens before, during, and after that purchase—every aspect of doing business with you, from your hours of operation to convenience features to whether your customers can reach you by e-mail, phone, text or in person. It's the sense of *hospitality* that people feel when they are doing business with you. And it is a truly holistic experience. It's a 360-degree proposition, including what happens *after* the people become your customers. Customers' impressions of you and your product or service depends on the total experience. The experience is what they'll remember, because it's about how you made them feel. We have all heard stories about people who wanted to buy something so much that they were completely sold on the product before they went about acquiring it. But then they experienced something awful or maybe just something that let them down and disappointed them, and *that's* what they remember. It's what they talk about and share with others.

A 60-something friend of mine recently switched over from an Android phone to an iPhone. My friend couldn't wait to get his new iPhone; he was completely and totally sold on the product before he bought it. But he had a terrible experience when he went to get it. No one in the store even acknowledged his presence for nearly half an hour. All of the associates in the store were in their 20s and ignored him. The store wasn't particularly busy, but the younger employees didn't greet him or offer any help. Perhaps they assumed that if he needed help, he'd ask for it. My friend isn't particularly "hip" or stylish or tech-savvy, and perhaps they ignored him for those reasons, too. Who knows? But the fact is, my friend felt alienated and uncomfortable, not welcomed and appreciated. He chalked it up to his age and the four decades of age difference between him and the store associates. He still purchased the phone and he loves it, but he tells *everyone* about how awful his experience at that particular store was—because despite the fact that he likes the product, the *experience* is what he remembers.

Consider as well that the magic was in the product in this example. It could have been sold from a vending machine and my friend still would have bought it. But how many products are that special? How many are the "only one that will do?" Nowadays, not that many. We have entered an era where products are becoming increasingly alike and more widely available, and with more standardized pricing. This makes it even harder to differentiate yourself, your business, or your product or service, because there are so many others that are similar. That's the bad news.

The good news is that what will set you apart from the sea of sameness is providing a great customer experience—and what's great about *that* is that it doesn't have to cost a fortune. You just have to really get to know and understand your customers, their needs, and their desires and figure out how to deliver service in the way that *they* want, that is, in a manner that's important to *them*. It's not about what you want. It's about what *they* want. And if "they" are different from "you," then this book will be the guide to showing you how to deliver a great customer experience to people not like you. And in so doing, you'll take business away from your competitors who don't take the time to learn about different customers.

Some even better news is that there are real, tangible, measurable business benefits to providing a great customer experience to diverse customer groups. Here are the top three benefits to your business:

1. **Sales. Sales. *Sales*.** I make you this promise: if you craft an exceptional customer service experience for different types of people not like you, your business will grow. You will have more sales and profit. It's guaranteed to work, because people spend money on what they value. And a key part of their values is how you make them feel, how you respond to *their* needs and wants, and how you serve them and treat them. So if you deliver an A+ experience on each of those points, you will close more sales, sell more products, retain more customers, foster greater loyalty, and generate referrals. I promise you outstanding sales results. Here's proof:

   I am friends with Ron Schwartz, the dealer principal at Cowboy Toyota in Dallas, Texas. Ron has always been focused on providing customers with a phenomenal experience—and he has always been successful because of that. Cowboy Toyota is located in a very diverse part of Dallas, with a large Hispanic population that lives within miles of the dealership. Yet just 5 percent of their sales were to Hispanic customers when Ron bought the dealership six years ago. He immediately recognized this opportunity to grow business and better serve the local community. But he knew that he first had to create a customer experience that would really "put the welcome mat out" for Hispanic car and truck shoppers.

   To do so, Ron hired bilingual associates for *every* part of the dealership, not just sales. After all, he reasoned, if you prefer to speak Spanish when you buy your new car, why wouldn't you also prefer to speak Spanish when you bring the vehicle in for an oil change? Ron added bilingual associates in every department, kept Spanish brochures on hand for every vehicle, expanded their business hours to better serve Hispanics who work late hours and couldn't come in before 8 PM, and added bilingual signage throughout the dealership. He's selling the same products to Hispanic customers as he is to non-Hispanic customers. But his efforts let his Hispanic car and truck shoppers know that they are in the right place and that Cowboy Toyota wants to earn—and *values*—their business. And earn it, he does. Today, 35 percent of the sales at Cowboy Toyota are to Hispanic customers. And my friend Ron says that he can't imagine where his business would be without that 35 percent. By simply putting the welcome mat out and crafting a great customer experience for customers not like him, Ron has grown his Hispanic clientele from 5 percent to 35 percent in just a few years.

2. **Demonstrating corporate responsibility.** Companies were once simply expected to make and sell quality products and services that were safe and competitively priced. That was a winning formula in business for a long time. Although you still have to deliver all of that today, you and your business are expected to be good corporate citizens, too. *Corporate responsibility* means being a responsible member of your industry and, of course, your local community. You must lead by example and "do the right thing." You must set the standards and then uphold them. You must be accountable for your actions, and those actions must be *sincere*. In other words, you can't claim to support or market to diverse customer groups and then fail to serve them. You must be consistent in your value statements and your actions. You can't, for example, market to Hispanics and then not provide services that they're likely to value highly, such as bilingual personnel or extended hours or a family-friendly shopping and purchasing environment. As a business, you have a corporate responsibility to not just talk the talk, but also walk the walk. By creating customer experiences that clearly show you value all customers, not just those who are like you, you tangibly demonstrate your corporate values and that you take your responsibilities as a member of the local corporate community to heart.
3. **Great customer experiences set you apart from your competition.** And when a potential prospect is researching and comparing you and your competitors online, a key factor in deciding to do business with you may be how you work with diverse customer

groups. The availability of information today has profoundly—and permanently—changed the business game. Nothing is hidden anymore. We all have access to pretty much everything we might want to know about. And today, customers want to know about *who you are*. They can and will check you out and judge you based on what they find. And they can learn many things about you, aside from your products and services, that will shape their impression of you and either turn them on or turn them off. Do you hire a diverse team of associates? Do your executive ranks reflect that diversity, or are you just paying lip service while the company is run solely by older white males? Do you make an effort to be green and take care of the environment? Do you donate your old computers to a local school or nonprofit organization? Do you give back to the community by volunteering for the occasional highway cleanup? These are all things that people can and will discover about you. And ultimately, each of us wants to do business with the "good guys." We feel good about ourselves when we make purchases that reflect our own values. So the more you cater to diverse customer groups and what they care about, the more connected to you those customer groups will feel. And this is a powerful weapon in your arsenal when battling tough business competition.

The best part of crafting a customer experience for people not like you is that you can control it. As a businessperson, there are a lot of things beyond your control that may affect you. You can't control the economy. You can't control the stock market. You may not have any real control over the cost of goods and labor. But customer service is the one thing that is *100 percent in your control at all times*. The variable in the customer sales equation that matters most of all is the one that you can control. Isn't that great?

You can't control the economy, the stock market, or even the cost of goods and labor, but you control the customer experience at all times.

It's also a challenging task to hire, train, and staff with the kind of people who will deliver a great customer experience. But it's a challenge you must tackle, because at the end of the day, *people* craft the experience your customers receive. And you, as a businessperson, must lead and guide your staff in recognizing that diverse customer segments are good for business. This book will help you lead your staff in the direction of diversity by teaching specific tactics and approaches that will provide you with a solid platform for providing the best customer experience for people not like you.

This book is not focused on the basics of good customer service. There are plenty of other resources out there on that topic, and I am assuming that you already know those fundamental things. This book is for the businessperson who is smart and forward-thinking enough to recognize that customers are changing; they're becoming less homogeneous and more individualistic and distinctive. This book will give you a simple, effective road map for how to take care of the customers you have, appeal to the ones you don't have, and delight and engage *all* of them. It's what you need now, and it will strengthen your business. So let's get started.

CHAPTER 2
Technology Armed Consumers with Mighty Big Bullets

For more than two decades, I worked in the automotive industry for top global ad agencies on major automotive accounts such as Nissan, Subaru, Lincoln-Mercury, and Toyota. Over those years, I watched that industry completely change its approach to serving auto buyers. First, the Internet brought massive, fundamental changes in the way people shop for cars and trucks. When I first started in the industry in the late '80's, auto shoppers used to have to go to a dealership, look at the selection, talk to a salesperson, then drive to another dealership, and begin all over again, just to compare vehicles and deals.

Then, suddenly, they could shop online. They didn't have to run all over town and spend a full day traveling from dealership to dealership to learn what was available, what the listed prices were, what vehicle options were available, and so on. Almost overnight, it seemed, auto shoppers could conduct significant comparison shopping in their pajamas at home and could narrow down their choices before heading to a dealership to finalize the purchase.

The next revolution took place when auto shoppers were able to "build" their own vehicles. Previously, the auto manufacturers built the cars and trucks that they believed would be best sellers—the vehicles they thought people wanted, in the colors that were most popular and with the features and options they assumed most people wanted. But consumers wanted to equip their new automobile with the options *they* chose, not ones that someone chose for them. Advances in technology made customization of options a viable possibility.

Technology is at the root of these fundamental shifts. It provides us with the ability to gather the information we want and need, when we want it, and it makes it possible for us to check out what the competition is offering and how their products, services, or prices differ. It also allows us to craft, for ourselves, a purchase that meets our unique desires.

Technology enabled consumers to get what they wanted, when they wanted it, and they became more vocal about their desires. They started providing *feedback*, and saying, in essence, "I like the way these jeans fit, but I wish they came in a darker wash," or "I hate trying on bathing suits. I wish I could try them on in the privacy of my home and see what I look like from all angles."

Once people were able to communicate with the companies that make the products or provide the services they want, there was no stopping them. And why would you want to stop a dialogue with your customers? If you can talk with your customers and prospects, you are more attuned to what's on their minds, what they need, what they want to spend money on, and what the subtle shifts in their tastes and preferences are. Interacting with your customers through social media channels such as Facebook or Twitter can only make you a better business and a better businessperson.

Another profound shift was taking place at the same time: the ever-growing diversity among people and within communities. It wasn't a coincidence that these two phenomena occurred at the same time; it happened because *technology feeds diversity.* Technology connects us in ways previously impossible—in real life or in cyberspace. We can share ideas, form relationships, and spark creativity. This connectivity and sharing fosters diversity, because it causes us to realize that there are groups of people who have differing perspectives and different opinions than our own. You also learn that people share common bonds—and whether those bonds are similar backgrounds, values, or interests, they often draw people together.

Take moms, for example. Women with children may be vastly different from one another in many ways: age, income, religious beliefs, parenting styles. Yet they bond over the shared experience of *being a mom* and all the responsibilities that accompany that role. The common thread of child rearing is greater than the many differences that a group of moms may have among themselves.

Technology feeds diversity. Sharing ideas with others sparks creativity and creates different perspectives.

When you broaden the circle of people you connect with, you'll inevitably form relationships with those who are different from you but with whom you have something in common.

Our diversity, coupled with technology, has fostered specific demands and created specific communities. Let me give you an example: if you are an environmentalist and you care deeply about planet Earth and conserving resources, you can easily find people online who share your values and views. You can connect with them through Facebook, chat rooms, blogs, specific events, and general conversation. You can talk with someone in India or China just as easily as you can with someone in Tulsa, Oklahoma. And as you connect with others who share your values, they will share with you their recommendations on companies, brands, products, or services that may be relevant to you and that conform to your mutual interest. They'll also tell you about the products and services that *don't* conform to your values or interests.

This is important, because although we get information from many sources today, the source we trust most is our circle of friends. They are the ones who have our best interests at heart, who know us best, and who know what we want, need, and care about. They're not trying to sell us anything (usually). They're simply trying to point us in the right direction.

One of my friends recently e-mailed me about "green burials." I know this is a bit of a morbid topic, but she and I had been discussing death and we shared with each other what we wanted to happen to our remains. She stated that she wants to be buried but expressed that she was conflicted about this, because cremation is viewed as more environmentally friendly. She's very conscious of natural resources and committed to preserving the environment. She weighs every decision she makes—from the clothes she buys to what kind of packaging her food comes in—based on its potential impact on the environment. She has a wide circle of friends and acquaintances who share her values and feel the same way. Despite her commitment to the environment, she just can't bring herself to be cremated.

Her online community of fellow environmentalists and conservationists had discovered and recommended a green burial service to her. A green burial is about what you *don't* buy. There's no chemical embalming and no casket or coffin. The body is buried in a shroud or simple biodegradable box, such as cardboard. There is no cement vault for the grave. She is looking into this type of burial and will probably make arrangements for herself with this "product," something she never would have known about if her friends hadn't filled her in on this new trend. Her online community shared and recommended an option for her that fits her values. They don't make any money from this; they just have her best interests at heart. It was technology, via her online circle of like-minded friends, that led my friend to research (and probably buy) a green burial.

Having connections to dozens or hundreds of people who share your interests, views, and values is powerful, because although the online community can giveth, it can also taketh away. Here's a different example:

If you are a breast-feeding mom, even simple things like running errands can be a challenge. You have to be able to feed your baby when he or she is hungry, regardless of where you might be. Some places are very breast-feeding-friendly, but others are not. Most moms are very discreet when nursing in public, but it still makes some people uncomfortable to see a woman doing it.

Retail giant Target recognized this and offers the use of their fitting rooms for customers who are breast-feeding. Even if other customers are waiting to use the fitting rooms, the breast-feeding moms have priority. Furthermore, Target doesn't insist that women must use the fitting rooms to breast-feed. They simply let women know that the rooms are available for them. That's their policy, which, in principle, seems like a good one.

But having a mom-friendly, breast-feeding-friendly policy and making sure that your employees know about, understand, and support this policy are two different things. Target learned this with a painful lesson about insensitive employees who exposed them (pun intended) mercilessly online and created a huge consumer backlash. It happened when one woman named Michelle Hickman had found a quiet place to breast-feed her baby in a Houston Target store. Although Hickman was fully covered, several employees approached her repeatedly and told her to go into the dressing room. She chose not to. The employees harassed her, stared at her, and even taunted her with mild "threats" about how she could "get a ticket for doing that" in the store (which is untrue—a woman has the legal right to nurse in public in Texas).

Hickman called the Target corporate offices to complain. But she also took her complaint to Facebook, and within days, a national "breast-feeding sit-in" was organized online. Hundreds of outraged women from Minneapolis to Miami took their babies and breastfed them in Target stores and parking lots. Of course, this attracted the national news media, and suddenly, Target was painted as a very unfriendly place for new moms to shop. Since moms are a key part of Target's core customer group, this hurt their image badly.

The irony is that Target *isn't* anti-breast-feeding. They have a clear policy that's designed to make their breast-feeding customers *more* comfortable. The actions of a few ill-informed and insensitive employees made one woman's experience a bad one. But it was *technology* that spread the news of that bad experience around the country at lightning speed, inspiring women and breast-feeding supporters to stage a very public protest. Michelle Hickman's single encounter ignited a media firestorm that spread like wildfire—online.

Technology is wonderful in many, many ways. It affords us the ability to know more about the companies with which we do business, to comparison shop, to research products and services easily, and to do all this at no cost. But as Target learned, technology can also amplify the customer experience and send it ricocheting around the world. It's a terrific asset when that experience is good, but when it's bad, technology can make it apocalyptic. And suddenly, what should have been a private and sincere "We're sorry" from Target to Michelle Hickman becomes an embarrassing public relations and customer retention nightmare that plays out on a very public stage.

It can happen to any company or organization, even yours. Unhappy customers now have some mighty big bullets in their arsenal to fire at you. It used to be that the worst thing a customer could do was to sue you if they felt wronged. Today, they can take your company down in a public, brutal, and immediate manner.

In the next chapter, I'll show you an easy way to understand the key stages that your customers undergo when doing business with you. It will help crystallize how important crafting the customer service experience is at every stage and how that experience can differ from one group to another.

CHAPTER 3

The Purchase Funnel: Understanding the Customer Experience from Top to Bottom

The customer experience doesn't begin when someone shops at your store, eats at your restaurant, or becomes your client. That may be the point at which that person decides to lay the money down, but the customer experience begins *well* before that point.

We all make choices every day about where and how we will spend our money. We decide based on a number of factors, such as price, location, value, availability, need, timing, and more. Long before we ever open our wallets, we have gathered information and formed opinions about what we think we should—or want to—do. We weigh the purchase decision against our priorities and values and choose accordingly.

Sometimes this process is very quick and easy. If you feel like chewing gum, you go and buy a package of gum. Gum is widely available, is inexpensive, and comes in lots of flavors. There aren't really any consequences to making a "bad purchase decision" in this case, either. If you don't like the flavor of the gum you bought, so what? You're out, at most, two dollars and can simply try a different brand or flavor next time. You can make a purchase decision about something like gum pretty quickly, because there's not much risk; you don't have a whole lot on the line.

But suppose you are planning to move into a new home? That's a purchase on an entirely different scale, and not just from the monetary aspect. You might consider things like the commute to work, the quality of nearby schools, the crime rate, property taxes, whether the home needs improvements or updates, the neighborhood's look and feel, noise levels, resale value, and more. Given all these factors, buying a house is not a purchase most people would typically make quickly. You would do your research and explore your options before eventually making a thoughtful purchase decision.

A pack of gum and a home may be on opposite ends of the spectrum in terms of the amount of time and energy put into the purchase process. Yet people still do, in fact, undergo a *process*, and they move through a number of specific phases when they're deciding to buy something. And *every one of the phases* plays a role in shaping the customer experience. There's even a model called the purchase funnel that illustrates how we, as consumers, move from the very beginning stages, when we first become aware that a product or service exists, to the final stage of being an advocate for that particular offering.

THE PURCHASE FUNNEL

You might wonder why it's called a funnel. This is because in any consumer purchase or ownership process, there will be people who choose not to buy a given product or service for some reason. Maybe it doesn't meet their needs, or it is too expensive. Maybe the process of buying it is cumbersome and clunky (think badly designed online retail websites), so they give up. Maybe an associate was unhelpful, poorly trained, or downright rude. Maybe the product they want doesn't come in the size or color they need. There are countless potential reasons why people undergo the first several phases of the purchase process and then exit without purchasing. The funnel analogy works because there will always be more people who research, look at, or shop your product or service than who actually buy it. In other words, the top stages of the purchase funnel will always have more people in them than the bottom stages.

Figure 3.1 is an example of the purchase funnel. Although there are a number of versions and variations out there, I like this one because it shows that the customer experience doesn't *end* with the purchase. The customer experience encompasses the entire process, from the initial stage of awareness, all the way through to the ownership experience and hopefully, the repurchase stage. Let me provide an overview on how to think about this model and illustrate how the customer experience exists during each and every stage.

Awareness

Before customers can buy any product or service, they must first be aware of it. This top stage of the funnel is the first step in engaging

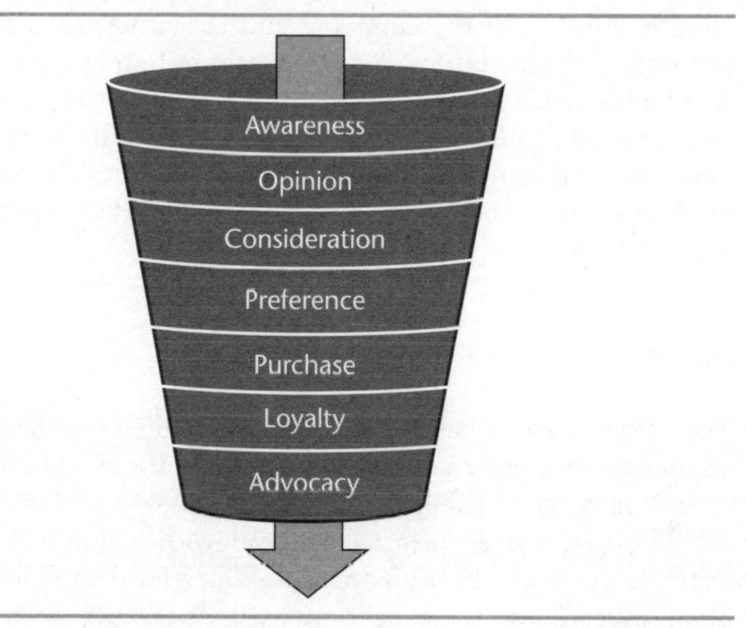

FIGURE 3.1 Purchase Funnel.

customers. You might be wondering how there can be a customer experience element to someone simply being aware of your product, service, or company. However, it's a key step; if the initial "awareness" is not well received, a customer can bail out of the funnel right then and there. Let's say that you're in the market for a new car. You suddenly start paying attention to the cars you see and begin to research and read about those that interest you. Along the way, you become aware of the Toyota Prius, a hybrid vehicle that is both ecological and economical. Because it's Earth-friendly, you might expect to see it on display at an Earth Day festival or some other "green" event. But suppose you saw it on display at a drag race or a monster truck rally? It would seem out of place there, not a very good fit. What does an eco-car have to do with a monster truck rally? In this situation, the customer's initial awareness experience of the Prius might be less than ideal.

As another example, suppose you like the way a cool brand of jeans looks. But then you learn that the company that makes them uses low-paid employees in impoverished countries who work in factories under deplorable conditions. That discovery could affect your perception of the company and cast a negative light on it, prompting you to fall out of the purchase funnel then and there. Remember the part in Chapter 1 about corporate responsibility and how consumers can learn about how your company does business? This is an example of the type of information that rarely used to come to light about companies but that is now readily accessible.

Opinion

This is the second phase of the purchase funnel; you begin to form an opinion of a particular product or service after you become aware of it. You begin to think about it in the context of favorable/unfavorable, inexpensive/expensive, high value/low value, and so on. For example, you could have an opinion about a local bank in your community, regardless of whether or not you do business with that bank. Perhaps the bank is family owned and has always supported local students with scholarships programs. Even if you're not a customer of the bank, you'd probably have a pretty favorable opinion of the bank because of its commitment to the community.

Consideration

People move quickly from the opinion stage to the consideration stage—or, they don't. If your opinion of the product or service is not favorable or appropriate, you drop out of the purchase funnel right there and never make it to the consideration stage. It's important to note that it's possible to have a high opinion of a product without considering it for purchase. For example, I have a high opinion of top-of-the-line cappuccino and espresso makers. However, I probably wouldn't consider one because I don't drink that much espresso and don't want to give up the counter space in my kitchen. If your opinion of the product that's relevant to you is positive (or even neutral), then you move into the consideration stage. This is the stage in which you are evaluating whether "this is for me" and consider the product or service from all aspects.

It's possible to have a high opinion of a product without considering it for purchase.

Preference

The next stage in the funnel is preference. Occasionally called intention, this takes place when you have moved past merely considering a product or service. You now actively feel a preference for the product or intend to buy it. It's imperative that the customer has a positive experience during this make-or-break stage; if he or she does, it is likely that person will move right into the purchase phase.

However, this is the stage where it can all go terribly wrong, too. We've all been there: you go to a store to check out a product you know about, are pretty sure you want, and are leaning toward buying. Perhaps you're just going to ask a few questions. If the experience at the store is positive—you interact with helpful, knowledgeable sales associates and encounter a clean store with a good selection of merchandise—you'll make a purchase. But if the in-store experience is less than ideal, you may not. A rude or ill-informed salesperson can destroy the chance to make a sale. So can a lengthy, confusing checkout process or a dirty store. Just because someone has a preference for a product or intends to buy that product is no guarantee that the purchase will be made. Remember the example of my friend who wanted the iPhone? He had a strong preference for that product and that was enough to compensate for the terrible experience he had in the store. But it could easily have gone the other way. Preference is a fragile stage. The customer experience is critical here.

Imagine how you can stack the deck in your favor if you used some techniques to provide a great experience to diverse customers at this stage. What might you do that could give you an extra edge? Suppose you have a bilingual sales associate who can assist customer prospects in their native language. Wouldn't that be a tremendous advantage in delivering an exceptional experience? Or suppose you are selling annuities and investments and you have brochures with a larger font to make it easy for someone older than age 50 to comfortably read them. The little things mean a lot, and they have a tremendous impact at the preference stage.

Purchase

The next stage, of course, is the purchase stage. Obviously, making sure that the customer has a terrific experience at this stage matters a great deal. Ensuring a positive experience here can take many forms: speed and efficiency, friendliness, hours of operation, even method of payment.

Several years ago, we worked on a project for a company called Eurosport that sells soccer products of all kinds online. A huge market segment for them is Hispanic men who play soccer, either on organized teams or just recreationally with friends. Many Hispanic men in the United States who are foreign-born lack credit. It takes a while to establish a credit history, regardless of how much money you make. Yet in order to buy products online, you typically must have a credit card.

Eurosport recognized this limitation for this substantial segment of their potential customers and removed that payment barrier by accepting money transfers from Western Union. Imagine what a great experience customers who lack a credit card can now have with Eurosport: they can do business with this online retailer simply because they can pay for their merchandise using Western Union. This little "tweak" has nothing to do with the merchandise they offer. It simply has to do with a method of payment, and it's a method that is highly relevant to and appreciated by a specific customer segment: in this case, a foreign-born customer who lacks credit.

What are the elements of your purchase process that can be tweaked to better serve diverse customers? Consider what it's like to do business with you at this stage of the funnel and then ask yourself if there are things you can modify to serve a specific customer. Here's an example of what I mean: I travel a lot and occasionally have some time to kill when I am on the road. One evening, I wanted to get out of my hotel room and do some window-shopping. I ended up in a nice store looking at handbags. The sales associate was great and showed me several bags, even though I made it clear that I was just browsing. Of course, she showed me one that I really liked and I wanted to buy it, but told her I was traveling and didn't have any extra room in my luggage to get it home. The sales associate immediately said, "We offer complimentary shipping. Would you like us to ship it home for you?" The answer was yes! In this example, an element of their purchase process fit the needs of a traveler.

Loyalty

If a customer has a great experience throughout the funnel, it will lead to the next stage: loyalty. A happy, satisfied customer is of course more likely to continue to do business with you. This is where you can demonstrate that you value your best customers on an ongoing basis and value their uniqueness. Here's a great example of fostering loyalty by letting a specific customer segment know that you understand and are responding to its needs.

When the Red Roof Inn hotel chain surveyed their business travelers, they found that most wished that hotel rooms had more electrical outlets. Most business travelers today utilize a number of different tech tools: mobile phone, iPad, laptop, and so on. It's important for them to be able to start the day with all of these gadgets fully charged and ready to go; therefore, they need multiple outlets to be able to charge all these items. The Red Roof Inn chain is currently renovating all guest rooms and has committed to provide a minimum of four more outlets in every room. Although any traveler can benefit from this upgrade, Red Roof Inn knows that business guests have lots of hotel options. They want to demonstrate to their core customers, their best customers, that they understand what they need when they're on the road. They also want to make it clear that they're working to make the Red Roof Inn customer experience for business travelers even better.

Advocacy

The last and final stage of the funnel is advocacy. This is the best stage of all because this is when customers are not just *satisfied* with your product, service, and the entire experience but actively *sell for you.* They tell everyone they know about you and why they love you. They influence others. They become walking and talking ads for you. They will even defend you or use persuasive skills when someone has a lesser perception of you. We all know people who advocate enthusiastically for a company or a salesperson. I am reminded of a conversation I had with friends about insurance. The topic was life insurance and one of my friends expressed that he didn't know where to begin to find a good agent to help him. Another friend, Robert, just couldn't say enough positive things about the insurance agent he uses. He went on and on about how his agent took the time to really educate him about different insurance products and crafted a recommendation for him and his family based on their needs and financial goals. My friend Robert was actively advocating for this particular insurance agent.

It's important to realize that *the advocacy stage never has to end.* The customer experience doesn't end here; in fact, these are the people you want to take care of, no matter what. You'll want to keep these happy and satisfied advocates loving you, because they are committed to the relationship with you. You can't put a price on the value of advocates. They are true ambassadors for you. This stage is the ultimate goal: you should be striving to make each and every customer an advocate.

In the next chapter, we'll dive into how you can tweak the customer experience throughout the purchase funnel to create more advocates for your business.

CHAPTER 4
We're Not "One Size Fits All" Anymore

Is it just me, or does it seem to you like business was easier "back then"? Depending on how old you are and how long you've been working, "back then" can mean anything from a few years to several decades ago. The fact is that business has changed *substantially* in recent years—for the better, in my opinion, since most businesses can serve their customers more rapidly and efficiently than ever before. We can communicate with customers in ways that weren't possible even a decade ago. We can access data that gives us more information about customer preferences and adjust our products, services, delivery, and communication to better fulfill those desires. We can have meetings with anyone in the world via Skype and can communicate with millions via Facebook and Twitter. We can learn—immediately—if customers are happy or unhappy with us, and we can take steps—immediately—to rectify customer service problems when they arise.

This is terrific progress; business and customers alike benefit from technology, analytics, refined business practices, greater transparency, and better communication. But with these rapid changes come challenges, especially in the area of creating a wonderful customer experience. There is tremendous pressure on businesses to make every customer not just happy, but *thrilled*. That challenge can be daunting. When you add into the equation that today's customers are very diverse, figuring out how to best serve people not like you can seem downright overwhelming. That might be why so many brands don't focus solely on how to provide a terrific customer experience for diverse groups of people. It takes a really forward-thinking company to realize and grasp that we are not "one size fits all"—and we don't want to be treated that way. We want to do business with companies that recognize that we, as consumers, are different and therefore want different things. We may have different expectations from one another, place more value on certain things than another would, express ourselves differently, or prefer to communicate in different ways.

In the past, catering to specific, diverse groups of customers certainly wasn't easy, if it was even possible at all. And for the most part, businesses didn't really have to. They sold a product or service, and once you became a customer, you were treated the same as every other customer. Maybe if you were a really important customer, someone who represented a lot of revenue to a company, they'd roll out the red carpet and give you VIP treatment. But the average customer was treated, well, in an *average* way; there was nothing special, distinctive, or unique.

CHOICE CHANGES EVERYTHING

Treating customers the same was fine then, because customers didn't have anything close to the multitude of choices that they have now. Everything was scaled back: there was one office supply store, one hardware store, perhaps one or two grocery stores nearby, only one way to see a movie (at the theater) and only one or two different movies (not 20 like today), only a few different kinds of soft drinks, a few brands of jeans, and so on. Today, we have numerous choices in virtually every product category. In some categories, such as soft drinks, there are *hundreds* of choices: regular and diet carbonated beverages, fruit juices, flavored waters, sports drinks, energy drinks, even "memory-improving" drinks. The same is true of office supplies. You can buy them everywhere: at the big-box office supply retailers, at Walmart or Target; at grocery stores; and in some cases, at gas and convenience stores. This kind of proliferation, whether it's the kind of product or service itself or the many places that you can get that product or service, leads to *choice*. And when customers have more choices, they become more *selective*. And when they become more selective, they will choose to do business with those companies, products, services, or brands that best meet their needs and desires.

When customers have more *choices,* they become more *selective.* And when they are more selective, they will choose to do business with those companies that meet *their unique needs.*

I say "needs and desires" because they are two completely different things but two sides of the same coin, just as marketing and customer service are. You really need both to be successful. Marketing addresses the need, but customer service addresses the desire. And although today's customers have many choices when they're looking to meet their needs, the opportunity is there for you to do more than that: *you can fulfill their desires as well.* And that's a powerful thing for your business to be able to do.

OMNI HOTELS GETS GUYS WHO TRAVEL FOR BIZ

The customer for Omni Hotels, in the broadest sense, is a traveler. But not all travelers are the same. Aside from the differences between business and leisure travelers, Omni Hotels found, shockingly enough, that men who travel for business hate ironing. Women apparently also dislike ironing, but men *despise* it. Yet they need to look their best for business meetings. Omni Hotels therefore tweaked the customer experience for men who travel for business by offering complimentary garment pressing for their Select Guest members. Although the service is available to all of their Select Guest members, they are catering to a specific *desire* of their most frequent male guests who stay there on business trips: the desire to have a freshly pressed shirt without having to iron it personally. When you are traveling, you need a comfortable, clean hotel room, but you desire the little perks and comforts that make your life easier.

MACY'S AND MORMONS

Here's another example of a brand that went beyond catering to a particular group's needs and met their desires. Macy's has department stores nationwide; like many department stores, they have an expansive housewares department. They have a vast selection of cookware, at every price point. But the Macy's in Salt Lake City also has a selection of larger-sized cookware, specially created for preparing larger quantities of food. Why? Because the largest population of Mormons in the United States resides in Salt Lake City, and a key tenet of Mormonism is larger family size. The average Mormon family living in the United States has four children, compared with two children on average for non-Mormon families.

A larger family means more food has to be cooked. The average-sized pot or pan may meet Mormons' cooking *needs;* however, it won't meet their *desire* to have a pan size that's suitable for cooking a larger meal.

Macy's doesn't *have* to stock this cookware. I am sure that most large families in Salt Lake City could get by with regular-size cookware. But Macy's has demonstrated that they understand Mormon family life: that these families are larger, make many home-cooked meals, and eat together. These customer insights mean that the local Mormon customer in Salt Lake City has a store that clearly recognizes their desires and values them as a viable customer group. Macy's is providing a useful, practical, realistic selection of products to the Mormon shopper and is therefore providing a meaningful customer experience that is unique to that local customer base.

Macy's has also demonstrated this same commitment to customer diversity in other stores and markets. For example, there is a large churchgoing population as well as a large African American population in Atlanta, so Macy's stocks more women's suits and dresses in white and a large collection of church hats. Because a significant percentage of the population in Minnesota is of Norwegian descent, they sell an electric iron used to make *krumkake*, a Norwegian waffle cookie. In Pittsburgh, they stock and sell *pizzelle* presses used to make Italian waffle cookies.

This localized approach, called My Macy's, is aptly named: customers in specific regions of the United States find products that are highly relevant to them, making it "their" store.

What does that have to do with customer service, you ask? The customer experience is broader than simply service. Service, to me, implies the human elements of respect, courtesy, responsiveness, efficiency, accuracy, and follow-through. But the customer *experience* goes beyond that in its totality. It doesn't matter how nice you are to me if you don't have the products that I want to buy. And it doesn't matter if you have the products I want if I don't like the way you force me to do business with you. Let me illustrate in the next section.

Not Just What, but *How*

Everyone who works makes money, and we all need to do something with it, which means having an account with a financial institution, whether it's a bank or credit union. These financial service providers offer products that may be largely the same. But *the way that someone wants to access* these services can be very different. For example, members of Gen Y have likely grown up with technology and the ability to do many things themselves, independently, online. These bank customers therefore probably want to be able to manage their accounts 24/7, wholly online. From bill paying online to making a deposit on their smartphones, Gen Y customers see no need to have to interact with a bank employee to complete their basic banking business. A top priority for these customers would be having a great mobile app for their phones. In fact, if the bank doesn't have a mobile app that makes electronic transactions easy for these customers, they may well take their business elsewhere.

My mother, on the other hand, is in her late 70s—and is a very different kind of bank customer. She doesn't want to do her banking electronically; she'd prefer to do it in person. She likes going to the bank and chatting with her teller, whom she's known for years. When she makes a deposit with that teller, she gets a paper receipt that she then goes home and files. She doesn't mind at all that this process is totally "old-school" and more time-consuming. She likes the familiarity and personal interaction she gets at her bank and has no desire to do her banking on her mobile phone. In fact, that would probably make her uncomfortable, because my mom is just not that familiar with apps and she probably wouldn't trust that they work properly.

There is no doubt in my mind that it's more efficient for banks to do business electronically with all of their customers. However, there are still customers who prefer the traditional way of banking, and they want to deal with a live person. Even though it might be easier, more efficient, and less costly for banks to serve the more tech-savvy customers, they still have to help those who are "not like them."

You'd have to cater to *both* of these types of customers if you were in the banking business, even though they are on opposite ends of the spectrum—in age as well as technology proficiency. In this example, the core product—banking services—is the same. It's the *way* that customers access the product or service that varies so widely. If electronic banking services were the only services available to someone like my mom, she'd find another bank. Remember, customers have *choices.* If you try to force them to do business *your* way, they may choose to do take their business elsewhere.

It doesn't matter if you have the products or service I want; I won't buy them from you if I don't like the way you force me to do business with you.

And this is where it seems that business "back then" really was simpler—because it was. Without technology advancements that enable us to do more or give us a more individualized experience, we were treated as if we are all the same. And if you didn't like that, you may not have even had the option of taking your business elsewhere, because there just weren't many "elsewheres." There simply weren't as many choices.

Thankfully, today, we have a wide range of options. It's certainly easier to get what we want, at a price we want to pay. But the customer experience is about more than that. Today, it's about giving people a memorable, meaningful experience that demonstrates that you see and recognize their uniqueness, that you value their diverse perspectives, and that you're committed to enriching their lives even though they may not be like you.

In the next chapter, I'll show you exactly how to do that.

CHAPTER 5

How to Think Like People Not Like You

People become easily intimidated when they start trying to cater to a customer group about whom they know little or nothing. Many businesspeople are so apprehensive and anxious about crafting these specific efforts for particular customers because they are scared of making a mistake. They don't want to offend a potential customer group by saying or doing the "wrong" thing. In addition, as I discussed in Chapter 2, they don't want to risk the potential for negative publicity and the subsequent media firestorm if they somehow blow it.

So if you feel this way, trust me—you are not alone. It's understandable that you'd feel doubt and trepidation. But despite the difficulties, this *is* the right journey to take, because crafting an outstanding customer experience for someone not like you *will grow your business.* It's what your competitors aren't doing (because they are scared or oblivious or both). And it's what will bring you incremental business and foster great loyalty among a new customer group that feels singled out in a positive, recognized, and highly valued way.

I don't want to imply that it's easy to get inside the heads and hearts of people not like you; after all, if it were easy, everyone would be doing it—and very few companies and brands are. However, it is *possible*, and that's where the huge upside potential is. If very few brands or businesses are taking this approach to the customer experience, then you can zoom to the top of the field just by tweaking what you already do! This wide-open opportunity is yours if you want it.

But before you can craft and then hone the customer experience for people not like you, you have to understand who they are, what they want (or don't want), what motivates them, and how your product or service may fit in with their lives. Once you answer all those questions, you can then ponder what it would be like to do business with you—*from their perspective.*

Let's look at the four steps in figuring out what different customers want from you and how to think like someone who is not like you.

STEP 1: ASK AND LISTEN

I talked in the last chapter about how Omni Hotels now offers free ironing to their most frequent guests. Although this amenity is available to any member of their Select Guest program, the *insight* and *idea* for it came from actual conversations that Omni had with men and women who travel. They simply asked customers what they hated about traveling and what they wished they could have. They conducted a survey of business travelers and found distinct differences between what male and female travelers wanted.

Males tended to have more extreme feelings about ironing than females. Although 71 percent of women agreed that ironing clothing was a "pain and chore" compared with 57 percent of males, Omni Hotels' study found that women are less likely to avoid it. In other words, women don't like ironing, but they do it anyway.

Men, on the other hand, take their adverse feelings for ironing a step further, with a full 20 percent claiming that they "hate" it. Overall, men are more willing to *take actions to avoid ironing:* steaming wrinkles out by hanging clothes near a hot shower (51 percent) or purchasing new wrinkle-free clothes for a business meeting or buying a new shirt while traveling to avoid ironing (51 percent). I chuckled a bit when I read these statistics. More than *half* of the men who travel for business are buying specific clothing or steaming their clothes, just to avoid ironing! That's an active dislike of a necessary task from the majority of one of Omni's prime customer segments.

So isn't it just *brilliant* that Omni Hotels would relieve these customers of a chore they despise? What a simple idea and relatively small service tweak! Yet the *perceived value* of this service is immeasurable. Business travelers have so many choices for hotels, and you've probably noticed that most hotels are clustered together within close proximity to each other in most cities. On top of that, many are priced within just a few dollars of their competitors. If you're holding a business meeting near a dozen hotels that offer similar rates within a 3-mile radius, then getting an extra "perk" that enhances your experience at one particular hotel could easily be the deciding factor in choosing where to stay.

Omni Hotels could have just "guessed" at what business travelers wanted. Or they could have brainstormed ideas and come up with various perks they couldn't even be sure customers would want, maybe a free muffin with their coffee or something like that. But by asking—by conducting a survey of actual guests—they uncovered a gem: an insight around which they could build an entire initiative. Not only did the complimentary ironing eliminate their best customers' biggest "dislike," it gave them an entirely new feature to market! Their Select Guest program is designed to cultivate and foster loyalty and repeat business. As many frequent travelers can tell you, most hotel loyalty programs are essentially the same: you earn points for stays, which eventually you can redeem for a free stay. Although that's great, hotels easily get lost in the "sea of sameness"; after all, if everyone has a similar program, it's hard to make yours stand out. But by offering a perk that addresses a specific customer segment's needs or desires, you demonstrate that you "get them"—and, quite possibly, may be the only one that does.

And the only way that Omni Hotels uncovered this gem, this not-so-insignificant insight about how men hate ironing, is that *they asked.* They did it in the form of a survey, but really, it's the same thing. If you ask people who are not like you what they want, you'll be amazed and pleased at just how eager they are to tell you. And you don't have to conduct any kind of formal research to uncover valuable customer information like that. Research is great if you have a budget for it, but many small and midsized companies don't. This shouldn't stop you from finding ways to talk to people and ask what they like, dislike, want, and need.

If you ask people who are not like you what they want, you'll be amazed and pleased at just how eager they are to tell you.

I recently spoke at a beer conference and met Dick Leinenkugel, president of Leinenkugel Beer. His presentation made a big impression on me because he talked about the importance of *talking to your customers—and your prospects.* Leinenkugel's brewery is a small one by brewery standards. They are based in a small town in Wisconsin and make wonderful craft beer, but they compete against huge companies such as Anheuser-Busch InBev and MillerCoors. They are very successful, but you can imagine what it's like to compete day in and day out against breweries that have enormous global marketing budgets, huge research and product development budgets, and so on.

Dick Leinenkugel talked about how his brand's sales force spends time talking with bartenders on their sales routes. They ask them questions about what customers are drinking and what they think of different beers, flavors, and promotions. They get many of their customer insights and ideas from these bartenders. After all, if you're sitting in a pub having a drink after work, chances are, you're going to chat with the bartender. So bartenders hear *everything!*

Seasonal promotion is crucial in the beer business, because people celebrate holidays and events by going out and having a drink with friends. Imagine the leg up a small brewery can have over a large one by asking the local bartenders what they are hearing from customers and then crafting a promotion around that insight to meet those customers' needs.

For example, Dick told me that the summers in Wisconsin are beautiful but short. Many people try to spend as much time at the hundreds of lakes as they possibly can, soaking up the great weather and enjoying "lake culture": swimming, waterskiing, jet skiing, fishing, and more. Beer fits in perfectly here. But with a limited promotional budget, Leinenkugel must spend its dollars wisely and make sure it is getting maximum bang for the buck. So based on input from bartenders who told them that customers who loved water sports wanted a light, refreshing beer that would be great for summer afternoons, they created a specific brew called Leinenkugel's Summer Shandy. Their lake-loving customers wanted a beer that wouldn't be heavy or slow down their active lifestyle. The Summer Shandy tastes clean and light, almost citrusy, and is one of their most popular flavors. It's brewed and available only for the summer months, which makes it very special and much in demand. This product adds to the "customer experience at the lake" by being a beverage that tastes right and satisfies the desire to have a beer while staying active outdoors.

Here's another example of learning a great deal just by asking and listening. A bank in the Midwest is situated in close proximity to a meat processing plant that employs thousands of local people. The plant hires many immigrants who have recently arrived from other countries where the language, culture, and norms can all differ dramatically from U.S. culture. The bank wanted to earn the business of the plant's employees, so they came up with a great idea: to provide mobile check cashing services on-site at the plant on payday. By being in front of hundreds (perhaps even thousands) of employees every two weeks when they got paid, they knew they'd form relationships that would lead to customer growth with additional services besides check cashing.

But even with this innovative idea, the bank was struggling to reach a large number of employees, specifically those from Sudan. (This particular plant had a large workforce from Sudan.) Try as the bank might, nothing seemed to be working. However, the woman who ran the bank's mobile check cashing operation managed to identify an influential Sudanese employee, just by consistently showing up at the plant every couple of weeks. She could tell he was a leader by observing how others treated him. He was an opinion leader, and people flocked to him and sought his advice. One day, she asked him why so few of the Sudanese employees were using the bank's free check cashing service. The influential man told her that, in Sudanese culture, most men don't do business with women. Their highly defined gender roles dictate that women perform household duties and have children, not work outside the home. Therefore, the Sudanese men who worked at the plant were not comfortable doing a bank transaction with a woman. To many of them, it was not only unfamiliar; it was wrong.

The bank understood the culture chasm, and they could have easily solved the problem by replacing their hardworking, effective female employee with a man. But the bank didn't want to abandon their values and principles just to gain a few new customers. The woman responsible for the mobile check cashing operation was a valued employee who did a great job; they weren't about to just yank her out of her role. So they struck a great compromise: they asked for a meeting with the clearly influential opinion leader among the Sudanese workers. They explained that they understood how things worked in Sudanese culture—that most women don't work outside the home and certainly not in financial services. But they also explained that, in the United States, women *do* work outside the home—and that this is a cultural norm in the United States.

The bank assured this man and his group that they valued them as potential customers and had a variety of products and services that would benefit the employees. They discussed mutual respect for cultural differences and let these potential customers know that they would accommodate the Sudanese culture by adding a man to the check cashing team. This meant that anyone who was uncomfortable working with a woman would have options. But the bank also made it very clear that the woman on the team, Martha, would *stay* on the team. They attempted to show that when two cultures with different perspectives converge, both sides must come together to find a mutually beneficial, workable solution.

And their approach worked! By engaging in respectful conversations and having a true desire to build bridges with people not like themselves, the Sudanese employees and the bank found a way to work together. As the Sudanese employees have become more accustomed to U.S. culture, they have also become more comfortable with Martha—and the bank added hundreds of new customers. None of this would have happened if the bank hadn't talked with the plant's informal employee leader. By simply asking, "What's holding you and your fellow employees back from doing business with us?" they learned of the issue and were able to develop a feasible solution based on compromise and mutual respect.

It's fairly simple: to learn more about people not like you and how you might tweak your product or service to enhance their experience, you just have to ask! Strike up a conversation with people in the group you want to get to know better. Ask them about what they like or don't like, and *listen carefully* to their responses. You'll almost certainly come away with a great idea, a key insight, or an issue you may be able to solve for them. But you'll never know if you don't ask.

One last thing on this topic: don't be shy or intimidated about asking people about their preferences. Most people *love* to share their opinions; it's just that companies and brands rarely take the time to ask. It's very flattering when a brand asks a customer's opinion on something. It validates you. It's a terrific place to start to learn more about people not like you.

STEP 2: PAY ATTENTION TO TRENDS

Two trends are simultaneously taking place across the globe: culture is becoming more casual, particularly in the way we dress, and fewer people are active in churches and houses of worship. I'm not sure these two trends are necessarily connected, but one certainly has an effect on the other. Let me explain.

We dress more casually than ever before. In many cities and communities, you can pretty much go anywhere—a museum, a restaurant, or the movie theater—in jeans and a T-shirt. But one place that people have always felt the need to "dress up" is at church. This habit is rooted in respect and tradition; there's even a quaint old-fashioned expression that captured the expectation: to wear your "Sunday best."

At the same time that our culture is becoming more casual, churches and other houses of worship are reporting a decline in members and those attending services. In Sanford, Florida, the pastor of Church at the GYM, Ron Williams, noticed this trend and adapted his approach to gain new members. As the Baptist church's name implies, he holds services in a gymnasium. He stated that when he would invite people to attend his services previously, they would often say no and say, "I don't have any clothes to wear." He called this a "stained-glass barrier" for people who might not be comfortable in a traditional church. To make people more comfortable, he even wears jeans himself. Many attendees in the warm climate of Florida wear shorts—and that's okay with him. He also welcomes clothing types like urban wear and biker gear.

Ron Williams doesn't care what you wear; he just wants you to attend and be comfortable. And it's working: Sandy Adcox, a 38-year-old interviewed by *USA Today* on this subject, said she hadn't been to church services in 18 years before attending Church at the GYM in March 2011. She hasn't missed a service since and stated, "I've never in my life been so comfortable in a church. It's so warm and welcoming." Church at the GYM even holds baptisms in members' pools, events that often turn into backyard barbecues that everyone enjoys.

Nontraditional churches are finding success with a new segment of potential members: the "unchurched." Younger people, in particular, tend to be more unchurched, and many churches want them to receive a message of faith. So they are adapting to the trends that young people want: an informal, accepting, and tolerant environment.

Bridge church in Flint, Michigan, is located in a strip mall and recently opened a tattoo parlor. Pastor Steve Bentley said, "We want to be relevant to people's lives." They use video clips to illustrate their message and make it more engaging to a generation raised with information and communication via multimedia. As Bentley explains, "We break with tradition, but we don't break with Scripture."

By paying attention to trends and what people want, these pastors were able to find a great way to tweak the church experience. If younger people want a less traditional stained-glass experience, why not give it to them? Aaron Coe, of the North American Missions Board, said, "We don't believe the building is the church. The people are the church."

In the food industry, a common trend these days is gluten-free foods. The demand for these foods is soaring as many people have found they can't tolerate gluten, a protein composite found in foods processed from wheat, in their diets. These people are actively buying products without gluten. If you own a restaurant or café, why *wouldn't* you want to enhance the customer experience for your gluten-sensitive customers by adding a few gluten-free choices to your menu?

A friend of mine, Katie, is highly allergic to gluten. We share a great circle of mutual friends and like to grab a bite to eat as a group whenever we can. Many times, Katie's gluten intolerance has been the deciding factor in selecting a restaurant—but not because the restaurant offers gluten-free items. When in doubt, as a group with Katie, we opt for Mexican food because she can have corn tortillas (instead of flour tortillas) and can eat something simple like black beans and rice and chips and salsa. But what if the group doesn't feel like eating Mexican food? The easy and best solution is to find a restaurant that includes a few gluten-free choices in addition to their regular menu so that a group or family eating out doesn't have to make a decision driven by just one person's dietary needs.

Pay attention to trends and modify the customer experience for people who may not be like you. It *will* grow your business.

STEP 3: OVERCOME BARRIERS

The less formal church environment is a great example of not just following trends but also *overcoming* barriers, specifically, the perceived barrier of "I have nothing nice enough to wear."

But the biggest potential barrier to understanding how people who are not like you think is that, quite simply, *you are not like them.* I'm not trying to be flip; it's so obvious. The only lens that I have with which to view the world is my own; I can see things only through my eyes, via my experiences, values, and priorities. I have no idea what it's like to be a man, to be in a wheelchair, or to be 80 years old. I have no idea what it's like to be Asian or in the military. You get the idea. Each of us has to work hard to break out of our comfort zone to tap into a market segment that is not like we are. That comfort zone of ours is a big barrier. We know what we know, and most of us are a little uncomfortable with what we *don't* know. And when it comes to our business, we don't want to make a mistake, do the wrong thing, or offend or upset anyone.

So here's the fastest and easiest way to overcome that barrier: *hire diversity.* Employ people who are *not like you.* It might sound simple, but it's the opposite of what most business owners do. Most business owners and managers hire people who are very much like them, which is understandable. If you are like me, then chances are that we'll get along pretty well. We will probably have similar backgrounds, experiences, or values, and these will lead to similar expectations of each other. We will probably look at problems and opportunities in a similar fashion. It will make my job a lot easier if you're like me, because we will be on the same page.

But to create a customer experience for people not like you, you must actually *enlist the help* of people not like you. If you hire someone who is different from you—whether in gender, age, culture, race, ethnicity, or lifestyle—you'll gain tremendous insight into how others like them think. You'll learn valuable information that can come only from someone with a different perspective.

To create a customer experience for people not like you, you must actually *enlist the help* of people not like you.

For example, my company has done a number of different consulting projects for insurance company State Farm over the years. They have a terrific brand and a vast network of agents, many of whom have been with the company for a long time. They're very, very good at providing their customers with exceptional service and a great experience. However, a lot of these agents are also in their 50s and 60s—and this maturity can sometimes put them at a disadvantage among younger Gen Y customers and prospects. And yet, Gen Y is who they want, because if they can bring in a customer in his or her 20s to buy auto insurance, they can likely also sell that customer renter's insurance and, someday, homeowner's insurance. And when that customer starts a family, they can sell him or her life insurance. The young Gen Y prospect represents *decades* of potential, ongoing business for them.

I was speaking with a successful agent in Albuquerque not long ago whose business was on pace to be up more than 60 percent for the year. When I asked her what she was doing to drive that kind of sales growth, she stated that she'd hired a woman in her early 20s several months prior. She had never had anyone that young on staff before. In fact, she told me she always looked for people with more experience—older people who'd been working longer—and generally avoided hiring younger applicants because they didn't have five years or more of experience.

However, this agent told me that her new young hire's approach to business was quite different from her own and was yielding *major* results. The young woman, Lindsey, used her activity on Facebook and Twitter to cultivate leads. Furthermore, she worked those leads through e-mail and texting, rather than on the phone. The agent shared with me that she was concerned at first, because Lindsey wasn't on the phone much and always seemed to be tweeting, texting, or Facebooking. Yet after a few weeks, she realized this is simply how Lindsey works and communicates. And that's how all of Lindsey's friends and colleagues—other members of her generation—communicate as well.

Subaru is a small car company compared with the big guys like Ford and Toyota; however, they have been highly successful in tapping into a particular customer segment: the gay and lesbian market. To provide a great customer experience for someone shopping for a new auto, you have to "put the welcome mat out" first by marketing to them and letting them know you want their business. For Subaru, that meant allocating a portion of their marketing budget for media targeted to gays and lesbians. The brand understood that if you market to a specific group, well, they'll respond. They also knew that many same-sex couples would go to Subaru dealerships to look at a new vehicle—and would want to encounter warm and welcoming dealers. They encouraged dealers to hire gay and lesbian employees and to be gay-friendly. The result is that today no other brand of auto manufacturer—of *any* size—has a greater share of the gay and lesbian market than Subaru does.

STEP 4: COMMUNICATE

The fourth step in learning how to think like people not like you is by communicating with them on an ongoing basis. This doesn't mean marketing or trying to "sell them" all the time. It means that you open up a dialogue with your prospects and keep it open so that you can remain abreast of what they do, think, and care about. You can do this by monitoring social media platforms and pages like Facebook and Twitter and by reading relevant blogs targeted to a specific segment and commenting on them. Toy manufacturer Fisher-Price does this effectively by following influential "mommy bloggers." These moms are so passionate about their children's safety and well-being that they blog about the companies and products that they like or don't like—and write posts that millions of other women see and read.

Fisher-Price wants to find out as much as possible about what these moms consider important. They want to know what's on their minds, what they worry about, and what they need. By following their blogs and reaching out to them with helpful (not sales-pitchy) materials, insights, tips, and facts, they enhance these moms' lives. For example, they provide moms with tips on how to keep their children active and healthy, something all moms care about. They foster dialogue to find out what moms look for in new toys. And by developing a relationship with the moms, they build trust. And isn't the cornerstone of all of the best customer experiences always trust?

Speaking of trust, it's important to communicate with customers and prospects so that they can keep up with what's going on with *you*. When customers feel ill informed or out of the loop, they don't feel valued, especially if they have a relationship with someone and then are surprised by their actions.

Susan G. Komen is quite possibly the most successful "brand" in the nonprofit fund-raising world. Their Race for the Cure for breast cancer is known and respected around the world. They have dozens of major corporate sponsors who put serious money (millions and millions) behind them to be affiliated with Komen and Race for the Cure. These corporate sponsors are very much "customers" of Komen, because Komen relies on them financially.

In 2012, Komen made a decision to remove funding from nonprofit reproductive and health services provider Planned Parenthood. The backlash and media firestorm was swift and unprecedented—public outcry based on customers' perception that the decision was inconsistent with Komen's stated value of caring for women's health and, specifically, breast health. Planned Parenthood conducts hundreds of thousands of breast screenings annually for low-income women, so Komen's decision to eliminate their funding seemed hypocritical to many. The beating that Komen took in the media was so brutal that the foundation reversed its decision within 48 hours.

But that's just the background story. My point is about *when* they informed their corporate sponsors of their decision. The Komen board made the unanimous decision to cut Planned Parenthood's funding on November 29, 2011. Yoplait, one of their largest corporate sponsors, received e-mail notification of the decision late in the day on January 31, 2012, the same day the story broke in the media.

That's unacceptable. You have a responsibility with any customer group, particularly those that may be unlike you, to communicate key changes to your business. Mutual respect, as well as simply good business practices, dictates that if someone is affiliated with you (as a corporate sponsor is), then anything that you do or say reflects on them as well.

Furthermore, people do business with companies because *their values align*. In this case, Komen's decision not only came out of the blue to Yoplait, it didn't reflect Yoplait's values at all. As a partner and corporate sponsor for years and years, Yoplait should have had the courtesy of knowing what Komen intended to do *before* they did it. Instead, they found out the same day as everyone else and were swept up into the negative public relations that ensued. It was not a very good customer experience for Yoplait.

These four steps will help you learn how to think like people not like you and grow your business accordingly. One of the best ways to do *all four of these steps*—on an ongoing basis—is to become active with the social media tools that are significantly shaping the customer experience for all of us. In the next chapter, we'll tackle low-cost and no-cost ways to harness the power of social media to further hone diverse customer experiences.

CHAPTER 6

How to Build Social Media into the Customer Experience

Because social media is vital to business today, I felt it was imperative to offer the best thinking from the most qualified and experienced social media professional I know. Jessica Levin is the president of Seven Degrees Communications, which focuses on using technology to build relationships and businesses. Jessica is a social media marketing strategist who works with dozens of major companies and consults with small to midsized businesses and associations. I reached out to her for this chapter and asked her to share the best tips for using social media to craft a better customer experience.

Social media is a gift to business. It's a godsend for the small or independent business owner, because the conversations that once took place only between people in private settings now occur more and more in public online environments. By "eavesdropping" on the right customer conversations, businesses can identify strengths and weaknesses in the products and services they—or their competitors—provide. Brands and companies can help people find answers to their problems and discover opportunities to develop solutions that may not already exist. Listening to online buzz also provides information about what your competitors are working on and allows you to react to industry threats. Essentially, you can think of social "listening" as a tool for market intelligence, consumer research, and customer service all rolled into one.

I talk with a lot of people who are confused by the role social media plays in business. Sure, everybody has a Facebook page these days, but a lot of business owners still struggle with how they are supposed to use social media for their business. They tend to think of it as an advertising channel, and I can understand why. It's the *media* in *social media* that makes people think of it in terms of advertising and marketing. But if you drop the word *media* from the phrase and focus instead on the *social* aspect, you'll be well on your way to developing a better understanding of how social media can help your business, particularly when it comes to providing an exceptional customer experience at every stage.

FIRST THINGS FIRST: THE NUTS AND BOLTS OF SOCIAL MEDIA AND THE CUSTOMER EXPERIENCE

Before we dive into the dos and don'ts of using social media to craft a phenomenal customer experience for someone who is not like you, it's important that we cover some of the essential points about how businesses today use social media to build and enhance customer relationships.

The term *social media* refers to an all-inclusive category encompassing a number of web-based and mobile technologies that create *interaction*, either between individual people or between people and a brand or company. The *social* designation is based on people's ability to connect and correspond with one another or with an organization; it includes applications such as Facebook, Twitter, LinkedIn, and Google+, as well as blogs, videos (YouTube), and other online communities.

Social media provides a valuable, effective, and *low-cost* way for companies to listen to existing and future customers, respond to their needs and concerns, and develop solutions or services that may not already exist. Although social media initially attracted a young, tech-savvy audience, they're no longer the only ones getting in on the action. A recent report by the Pew Research Center revealed that half of the social network users in the United States are older than age 35. Even if you are not using social media, personally or professionally, you must not dismiss it. It's the biggest thing to happen to business—and culture—since the Internet.

Social media is also the great equalizer, as it allows you to create and maintain online relationships with customers and prospects, regardless of your company's size. How can a small, individually owned coffee shop compete with an industry giant like Starbucks, for example? Fostering a loyal, engaged, and supportive customer dialogue online using social media is one way. Social media can be a viable and *realistic* approach to customer service for a company of any size.

Since social media is, well, *social*, the etiquette for businesses that use it has typically called for relationship building over direct selling.

After all, how many times would you go over to a friend's house if she tried to sell you something every time you stopped by? We are all exposed to an overwhelming number of marketing messages, every day—we don't need another pitch. What we need is a company, brand, product, or service that shows that they *get us*. Companies that take the time to get to know their audience and build a sense of community online provide a much better customer experience than those that simply promote themselves and their products and services. Although there is no right or wrong approach, you can create and build positive experiences for your customers by listening, serving, and connecting people.

Let's look at the five steps you need to take to make social media work for you to enrich the customer experience.

Step 1: Empower Your Community Manager

At many companies nowadays, the person who manages the social media communication is referred to as the community manager. That's because this person's job, or part of it, is to listen to and talk with the online community. Although community managers are often members of their company's marketing departments, their role extends beyond marketing; they are also responsible for responding to questions and concerns. After all, the objective behind using social media to enhance the customer experience is to create long-term relationships. Therefore, it's critical for the social media manager to have the authority to make and carry out certain decisions on the company's behalf. You can't measure the impact that social media has on your business solely by the number of sales obtained; you must also consider the exponential result of the *connections and relationships built*. Although closing the deal is important, the referrals and recommendations you can obtain through a strong online community can easily outweigh the amount of direct business closed.

With that perspective in mind, it's important that you select the right member on your team to be the "voice" of your company online. The ideal community manager or social media representative is knowledgeable about your organization's culture as well as your products and services. But perhaps, more importantly, that person must also have the maturity to deal with many different types of people and personalities, particularly unhappy campers. Your social media reps are *company ambassadors and troubleshooters;* they need direct access to the "deciders" in your organization so that they can take action to help a customer get a timely and accurate response or resolution.

Your community manager doesn't have to have all the answers. He or she just needs to be empowered to *get* the answers.

This does not mean that community managers should have free reign to do *whatever* they deem essential. But in order for them to be successful and effective, it's important that they be empowered to meet the needs of the community that they have helped to build.

Here's a good example: LINE-X is a company that does spray-on protective coatings for many surfaces, but a big part of their business is selling to pickup truck owners; they provide a top-quality spray-on bedliner. People are pretty passionate about their pickup trucks, and investing in a spray-on bedliner is an important purchase for them. LINE-X has a network of authorized dealers all across the United States, as well as a community manager named Cristin Liveoak who works in the company's marketing department. She's not a technician, a dealer, or a district manager. Yet she fields questions and comments from their Facebook fans (or "likers") every day. Periodically, she'll get a question—or a problem or issue—to which she must respond, even though she's not the person who will actually solve the problem. After all, she works in the marketing department. But since she's responsible for the *online customer experience*, she must be able to access the right members in the organization to help her resolve any customer issues that arise.

You can see how important empowerment is; imagine if Cristin went to a district manager with a customer complaint or spoke to a technician about a technical or chemical question and was ignored or dismissed. She wouldn't be able to do her job effectively. By empowering the community manager—and *making sure others in the organization understand why this role is so important*—you can facilitate a great customer experience. Community managers don't need to have all the answers. They just need to be able to *get* the answers—quickly and efficiently—from others who do.

Another example of something that Cristin and LINE-X do well is provide a personal connection: when communicating with customers online about complicated issues that require a few days to track down the best solution, she always gives them her name. This way, customers know that they're working with a real person. For example, Cristin recently encountered a customer on Facebook who had a series of technical questions. She responded with, "Hi Bob—thanks for your questions. I am going to get you the answers you're looking for, but I will need a little time. I will get back to you on this in two days. My name is Cristin and I wanted you to know I'm the person working on this for you." She does this faithfully whenever something is going to take longer than a day, and the company's Facebook fans always respond positively. Her personal touch—sharing her name—enhances the customer experience that much more and really instills confidence that LINE-X is on top of things.

Although a single individual may manage the online community in smaller businesses and organizations, larger companies often have a team of people who are charged with handling social media accounts. In either case, it's best if you identify on your social networks specifically who does what so that the online community knows exactly with whom they are dealing. We've all had the experience of calling or e-mailing a company and wondering if anyone is actually listening or will respond. The anonymity of that type of communication is frustrating, because, as a customer, you don't know if there's a specific person who is responsible for helping you.

An easy way to make a strong statement about how committed you are to your customers is to be clear that a *real person* is in charge of the social media communication. Post something like, "Jessica Levin is our Facebook Community Manager. Talk with Jessica about your experiences and let us know how we can serve you better. We're listening." And speaking of listening, that's the second step.

Use your name in your online posts to make the experience more personal and warmer for your customers and prospects.

Step 2: Listen

> Businesses used to have a small suggestion box near the door that mostly housed dust bunnies and an occasional piece of gum. Rarely would someone get back to you. But people can now make a post from their phone while they're sitting in your restaurant.
>
> —*Charles Nelson, President of Sprinkles Cupcakes*

You absolutely must listen online, because that is where you will find the unvarnished truth about what your customers and prospects think of you. I always say, "I am not afraid of the problems I know about. I am afraid of the ones I *don't* know about." How can you correct a misstep, resolve an issue, or change your business for the better if you don't know what people want, what frustrates them, or how they feel about doing business with you?

You can conduct online listening in a variety of ways; it can be simple or complex, depending on your needs and your resources. A basic approach to listening is to create a keyword search that's relevant to your business. (See Figure 6.1.) For example, a local coffee shop might want to receive an alert every time someone mentions coffee, tea, or Starbucks in cyberspace. One of the most popular social media management tools is HootSuite (www.hootsuite.com). This tool is based on a freemium model where it offers certain features for free and charges for others. HootSuite allows the management of multiple accounts and multiple social networks (Twitter, Facebook, LinkedIn, and Foursquare, to name a few). With HootSuite, users can post, schedule posts, filter accounts, and track click-through rates. By using HootSuite, you can set up a query for those terms and capture all mentions of any or all of them. HootSuite also allows you to drill

FIGURE 6.1 Example of Twitter keyword search for "coffee," "tea" and "Starbucks."

down by viewing only posts that are close to your geographic location so that you are capturing a local audience.

To take the example further, suppose you want to attract families with children to your coffee shop. You might then wish to add "kids" or "mom" to the search. Keep in mind that this is not an exact science and requires a bit of tweaking. There will be some time commitment—as well as trial and error—in keyword testing.

But once you've found those posts, you've found relevant customers who you can then engage in conversation or simply follow on whatever social network you are using. If you choose to engage them, consider a reply that is relevant *to them* and not totally self-serving. Commenting on something that they posted or that they referenced in their online biography can be a nice way to break the ice. However, if someone directly asks, "Where can I find a coffee shop in Anytown, USA?" you can certainly reply and suggest your venue. If they merely mention the coffee they are drinking, you might ask what their favorite flavor is, how they take their coffee, or something completely unrelated to coffee. It's important to remember that most people don't get engaged on the first date; there is an entire courtship process. Social media engagement is no different. You must take the time to develop and nurture a relationship. This is what allows you to turn someone who never knew your company existed into a loyal customer.

Remember that most people don't get engaged on the first date; there is an entire courtship process. Social media engagement is no different.

In addition to HootSuite, you can perform similar searches using Facebook and Google+. In addition, you can set up Google Alerts to scour the entire web; this is useful in identifying conversations taking place on blogs. You can conduct more sophisticated searches through premium services such as Radian6 and Vocus, which scour both online and traditional media for information. The tools available to monitor and measure online activity are always evolving and provide very detailed and refined results. But all of them will give you and your business a peek into the minds of the marketplace.

If you are using Facebook as a social hub, advertising can be an effective means of driving the right customers to your page and your community. Since members provide a great deal of detail about themselves in their profiles, you can develop Facebook ads to target a very specific market. In addition to basic demographic information, you can tailor ads for specific interests, activities, occupation, and beyond. Socially driven ads allow you to promote your page or business to people who have friends who are already members of your community, thereby creating a warm welcome. For example, Jason Blaine, a popular Canadian country music artist, used ads to support an engagement strategy. He targeted fans of other modern country stars as well as fans of major festivals that he was performing at to promote his new CD. The result was that people who enjoyed country music could discover a new artist in the genre. Although you might not have direct access to the personal profiles and the conversations that users are having, Facebook does the listening for you—and can help drive traffic your way.

Many industries and demographic groups have certain influencers with large and active online presences, including blogs. Connecting with, conversing with, and listening to these opinion leaders can be wonderful ways to break into new markets and get a feel for market trends. So how do you identify a person of influence? Service companies such as social media analytics company Klout attempt to categorize people based on topics that they frequently discuss; however, this is not a perfect solution for identifying true influence. Businesses that use this approach may need to spend some time researching and then engaging with thought leaders via social media. Influencers often convene and converge to share experience and expertise. For example, www.latinamombloggers.com helps Latina moms who blog connect with one another. If this were one of your key customer groups, or one you wanted to cultivate, this website would help you identify influencers among Latin moms who also blogged about their experiences.

Step 3: Serve Transparently

Before the days of social networking, an unhappy customer might tell three people about his or her experience. Now an unhappy customer can easily tell 3 million, with much less effort. The Internet has made it possible for disgruntled customers to broadcast their feelings about an organization to their entire online network.

That's the bad news. The good news is that companies now have the opportunity to instantly identify concerns and address issues. You should make it a policy and/or practice to proactively listen for people to mention your company name—and then have a strategy in place to address concerns online. As mentioned, you can do this by using tools like HootSuite, Google Alerts, Radian6, or Vocus.

Comcast figured this out in the early days of Twitter. People are very passionate about cable television, particularly if service is disrupted during their favorite show or an important sporting event. So when people started airing their grievances on Twitter, Comcast was there to help. With an empowered team of community managers, they respond to tweets in *minutes* and try to alleviate the problem. The community managers are friendly and professional, and even if they can't help customers themselves, they direct customers to the people who can. This response has been invaluable in helping them turn irritated customers into happy ones.

Popular online shoe and clothing company Zappos, known for "delivering happiness," always has someone available to respond to customer service issues via Twitter. And despite the fact that they have an excellent reputation for going above and beyond when it comes to providing satisfying customer experiences both online and via phone, their track record is not perfect when it comes to meeting the promise of delivering happiness.

In 2012, the company was the victim of a security breach that compromised customer information. They received a great deal of criticism for their limited commentary on the issue on their website and via Twitter. Although employees received news of the leak via a letter from Zappos chief executive officer (CEO) Tony Hsieh, the company refrained from further comment. It was difficult to locate information about the breach on their website. Based on how active their social presence is, many customers expected them to provide more information, but none was forthcoming. Although the company quickly recovered from the negative publicity, the experience serves as a reminder that crisis communication needs to be built into a social media plan.

You must consider crisis communication plans in your social media efforts, in case the worst happens. Customers want steady information.

A lot of companies have now configured themselves to allow customers to proactively contact them via social media when they have customer service issues. Social media is a public forum, however, and company representatives often take the conversations "offline" to address questions or concerns. This is where it's most crucial to empower your social media community manager. Few things are more frustrating to an already-unhappy customer than hearing that they must call the toll-free number for support *after* they've reached out for help via social media. If a customer is using social media to communicate with you, this indicates that this particular social channel is likely their preferred form of communication. They don't want to be redirected to another method simply because it is more convenient for your company.

Of course, this does not mean that the phone should not be involved at some point; sometimes having a conversation with a person and hearing a human voice is the only way to go. That's one way to take the conversation offline; e-mail is another.

However, companies big and small must face the fact that social media is the new normal way to communicate; it provides people with the ability to connect to anyone, anywhere, at any time. Even if your company has not traditionally had a strong online presence, you can still benefit by crafting a satisfying experience for customers who are not like you.

Step 4: Provide Direction

You can guide people to certain social media platforms (such as Facebook or Twitter) to help manage customer service. Socially savvy consumers generally know on which platform they're most likely to get a response, and they may try to reach your company there. Facebook implemented a messaging feature on their new Timeline format that allows people who "like" a Facebook page to contact that page's administrator. If your company chooses to enable this optional messaging feature, you need to be prepared to respond to messages.

Online grocery delivery service Peapod does a great job of using social media to handle customer issues. They recognize that people who have their groceries delivered are often too busy or unable to get to a grocery store, and they focus on providing convenience and personal service. Peapod's model emphasizes assistance that allows customers to exchange or refund items easily if they don't meet their needs. After all, they're busy people who don't have time to waste exchanging rotten tomatoes.

Since they're a web-based business, Peapod provides customer assistance via phone or e-mail. A flaw with this model is that the people who answer the phone are not always as empowered as the social media manager. This may explain why the messages that customers post to their Facebook wall often result in a better outcome than calls to the toll-free number do. One particular instance involved a customer's need to change a delivery time to within a few hours of Peapod's scheduled arrival. Although polite and professional, the customer service representative on the phone was unable to change the time. However, a message the customer posted on Peapod's Facebook wall got the job done.

What factors may have contributed to this? Well, traditional customer service agents are trained to handle high call volume with efficiency. A social media manager often comes from the marketing department and may feel a greater sense of responsibility to protect the brand. In addition, the *public nature* of these comments drives the need to produce a better outcome. These are all possible reasons why a social response to a customer service issue was able to satisfy a customer when the telephone channel could not.

The key lesson to learn from this is that customers should be able to achieve the same results and level of service regardless of the method of contact. Looking at these differences can assist you in refining your processes, whether they are social media-driven or traditional. If people are able to choose the communication channel that fits into their unique lifestyle, then they're more likely to be loyal to your business.

The public nature of comments drives the need to produce a better outcome.

Step 5: Connect

Creating customer experiences need not always involve your company, at least not directly. We have discussed the importance of building relationships and a sense of community. One vital aspect of relationship building requires that you become a true connector by introducing members of your market to one another, which will help them derive mutual benefit. Again, listening is essential; by paying attention to what your customers are saying, you have the ability to connect people who can potentially gain by interacting with one another.

What's in it for you? The payoff is that your company will quickly develop a reputation as an organization that puts *customer relationships first* and sales second.

If you have a product that people are passionate about, chances are that customers are already talking about your company or your competitors. Connecting can be as simple as introducing customers to one another because you know they share a common interest. For example, you might connect two people who drink only soy lattes and share some valuable resources about dairy-free products *in addition* to the ones that *you* sell. In other cases, a customer might be looking for a specific service that you don't provide. By connecting that person with someone who *does* provide the service they are seeking, you send the message that you value them as people, even if helping them find what they need doesn't directly benefit you in any way.

You can build brand loyalty by paying attention to what is important to your market—or a segment of it—and then figuring out ways to support those individuals. Suppose, for example, that you discover that you have *a large* number of customers who drink only soy lattes. Maybe they have a dairy allergy or choose to lead a vegan life or simply prefer the taste. By inviting them to join a group on Facebook or LinkedIn to discuss and share health tips, you show them that you are aware of—*and care about*—their preferences. You might post relevant information to the group to enhance everyone's experience, or you might just sit back as an observer and allow the community to form.

Businesses of all sizes, with all kind of budgets, can successfully serve their markets via social media. But how do you use social media to enhance the customer service experience for *diverse* customer segments? Following are some examples of how a small business, a medium-sized business, and a global enterprise use social media to create customer experiences for people not like them.

FOILED CUPCAKES: START-UP TO SMALL BUSINESS

Chicago-based Foiled Cupcakes wants their customers to be their friends because they know that it is easier to do business with people you know. Foiled has two target customer markets. The first is composed of professional services companies such as technology companies, law firms, accounting firms, and insurance agencies. Because customer retention is critical for these companies, many firms send cupcakes as a thank you to their clients. The second market for Foiled is bridal/wedding events. They take a personal and friendly approach in both markets, where relationships trump sales every day.

Foiled's model is to operate as an online business with no physical storefront. When Mari Luangrath started the company in 2008, she experienced some delays getting her website launched, which meant a delay in selling cupcakes. Someone suggested to Mari that she create an account on Twitter while she was waiting.

She took the approach that she would simply start having conversations with people in her local area and see what happened. Mari didn't start conversations on Twitter talking about cupcakes; she started talking about things that she was interested in, including shoes. Soon she established a rapport with her followers, who wanted to buy cupcakes from her. After several weeks, the website was ready and orders were flooding in. Mari had created an *experience* through her online networking before her business's virtual doors even opened.

The customer experience infiltrates the way that Foiled does business; they adhere to very specific policies. For example, they sell cupcakes only by the dozen, and they don't customize designs; however, they offer 18 different flavors in three varieties. And here's the remarkable thing: when they can't meet a customer's needs, *they happily refer them to a number of local bakeries that can.*

Foiled serves as an extension of a business by sending cupcakes to a company's clients or prospects, complete with a handwritten note and the company's marketing materials. Companies provide Foiled with a list of recipients, and Foiled does the rest.

Their customers who have ongoing needs can enroll in a program called Silver Elite, designed for convenience, quick response, and most importantly, the relationship aspect. Through Silver Elite, customers are assigned dedicated account managers whom they can call or text when they need an order sent. As a gesture of appreciation for Silver Elite clients, Foiled provides them with gifts to celebrate 3, 6, and 12 months of working together. Gifts include gift cards, dinner with the owner and account manager, and an in-office cupcake party. They also send cupcakes for their clients' birthdays and even for the special occasions of their clients' significant others, with customized messages of appreciation.

Foiled's culture of friendship and service is reflected in their online presence. They have grown active Facebook, Twitter, and Pinterest communities where they emphasize the importance of making people feel welcome and cultivating the new relationship. For example, they look at a new Twitter follower's bio to find something interesting about them to comment on. Foiled considers it crucial for them to open up a dialogue with people who like their brand.

For Foiled, selling takes a backseat to the customer experience. A big fan of the online game *Words with Friends*, Mari offered people who like her company's Facebook page a chance to compete with her for the chance to win a box of their seasonal cupcakes. This variety of cupcakes changes flavors every few months; so rather than simply announcing their flavors, Foiled created the *Words with Friends* cupcake contest. This not only helps to spread the word about Foiled, it also creates an *experience* for customers.

Pinterest, the social network site known for displaying vision boards with beautiful photos, is great for reaching the bridal market. Foiled follows brides who are located in their delivery area and comments on the photos they post. Although they never directly mention their products, they managed to secure eight wedding catering jobs in four months through Pinterest alone.

While Foiled is busy connecting with brides on Pinterest, they look to the more business-focused social network LinkedIn to reach some of their corporate clients. On LinkedIn, Foiled created a private, invitation-only group to which they invited local administrative and human resources professionals. The group's goal is to have members share information on how they are making a difference in their company. Members are prequalified to fit into the right target market for Foiled and must contribute to remain a member in good standing of the group. Foiled's only role is to serve as moderator and group owner. Although they have only 40 members, 60 percent of whom are Silver Elite, they have a high level of participation and are maintaining relationships with their best customers.

Regarding her social media efforts, Mari said, "There is nothing to lose by creating a relationship online. It takes less time and money than driving around, dropping off samples to prospects and clients in our delivery area, and achieves the same results."

HALLS DEPARTMENT STORE—MIDSIZED BUSINESS

Halls is a high-end department store located in Kansas City, Missouri, that was created in 1916 by Hallmark founder Joyce C. Hall. The store's vision was to be "first with the best in Kansas City," and they've always focused on delivering a "unique shopping experience defined by unparalleled selection, attentive personal service and not-to-be-missed events." Anyone who has ever shopped at Halls can attest that they do, indeed, deliver what they promise. Having such an established presence in the area, they have traditionally attracted a baby boomer and more senior clientele. Many members of younger generations have not thought of it as a place to shop for "their" style. Yet despite the store's reputation as a place for older, affluent shoppers, the reality is that Halls carries modern brands and has a strong sense of contemporary style.

Halls turned to social media to change the perception that younger people had of them and to convert young, professional, and stylish women into loyal customers. Halls has a dedicated Twitter team that does more than post about the latest shoes on sale. They take the time to identify professional, influential young women based in the area and connect with them in a meaningful way—which they do by communicating with them in their preferred social media format.

Katie Hollar is the 30-something chief marketing officer for top Kansas City, Missouri, law firm Lathrop & Gage and an avid Twitter user. Halls identified Katie as a target prospect, based on her status as a young, local professional with disposable income. The store began to follow her on Twitter and engage her in conversation. It's important to note that their conversations were not just idle banter; when Katie needed a pair of seersucker pants for her husband, for example, @HallsKC searched for the right pair, thereby saving Katie valuable time. For New Year's Eve, @HallsKC scouted shoes for Katie, sending her links and photos. As experiential events are a core value of Halls, they proactively invite people to store events and sales via Twitter on a regular basis. When Katie and her friend Marina were discussing skin care in regard to a special event they had coming up, @HallsKC invited them to come in to the store for complimentary facials and to have their makeup done, then profiled the experience on the store's blog, What the Chic: http://blog.halls.com/2011/01/girls-day-out-at-halls-with-katie-marina/.

According to Katie, "We felt like queens and will be loyal to Halls forever. We enjoyed our experience so much that we shared it on both Twitter and Facebook." Both women have vast numbers of followers and friends on both sites—and Halls now has two influential, stylish women touting their stores and service to thousands on their social networks.

TOYOTA SIENNA—GLOBAL

When you think of minivans, the top-of-mind image is no doubt soccer moms wearing "mom jeans." Indeed, this is the very image that may have led to the sharp decrease in minivan sales in recent years, as more and more families opt for SUVs that have a higher "cool" factor. Toyota understands this perception and is fighting it by positioning their minivan, Sienna, as the "Swagger Wagon." They launched a campaign that introduced a fictitious couple in their 30s and their two children known as the Sienna family, rapping about the Swagger Wagon. The original commercial developed into a series of TV commercials and a dedicated YouTube channel with videos that feature the family. Many of the videos are not only about the vehicles; they also show interviews with the family discussing "life," including how the couple met and the upcoming new addition to the family. The original video has received more than 10 million views and is available as an MP3 download or a ring tone at www.toyotaswaggerwagon.com.

The Facebook page acts more like the personal profile of Swagger Mom Rachel. It is filled with videos and photos of the family. In one video, Rachel encourages people to "like" the photos and make comments about her because it makes her feel pretty. However, Rachel is still somewhat humble and also wants to see the photos of her online friends and their families and encourages them to post pictures of them and their Swagger Wagon.

Toyota has created an online community around this couple, to whom many members of their target market—that is, families with kids—can relate. Many Sienna owners request their very own Swagger Wagon decal so that they can show the world that they are as cool as the Sienna family.

This online presence gives current and future Sienna owners a place to gather, discuss their minivans and their lives, or simply feel like a hip, modern family.

We've covered a lot of ground in this chapter. Let me leave you with six tips for using social media to create an enhanced customer experience:

1. **Follow your target market zealously.** Networks like Twitter and Google+ allow you to search for keywords and demographic information so that you can connect with tightly defined customers, including those who are not like you.
2. **Seek customers out.** Don't wait for them to come to you. You cannot limit customer experiences to those where *they* initiate the conversation. Create relationships with your customers on social networks *before* they need you.
3. **Keep it real.** Talk to people as a person, not a business. Even big organizations can build individual friendships. Emphasizing the importance of *customer relationships* over corporate messaging goes a long way in building loyalty.
4. **Utilize a management tool.** A variety of listening and management tools, both free and paid, are at your disposal. Evaluate the features and benefits of several and figure out which ones meet your goals. The following are great tools, but be aware that certain products change in this rapidly evolving medium:
   - HootSuite (freemium; good for small and large companies)

- Sprout Social (variety of plans for all sizes)
- CoTweet (larger organizations)
- Google Alerts (free basic keyword search of all web content)
- Social Mention (basic alerts similar to Google Alerts with social focus)
- Radian6 (advanced social and traditional media monitoring service)
- Vocus (advanced social and traditional media monitoring service)

5. **Remain flexible.** Social media changes quickly. It is therefore essential for you to remain abreast of changes so that you can be ready when your customers need you.
6. **Listen and respond.** Smart companies have *active listening campaigns* and proactively seek out people in their target markets with whom to make connections.

CHAPTER 7

Your Employees May Kill Your Business, Unless They Know How to Serve Customers Who Aren't Like Them

We've all heard the claim, "Your employees are your greatest asset." And although that's true in a general sense, it's *critical* when it comes to doing business with people not like you.

Why? Because the customer experience itself is different for different types of people. People who are older want very different things than those who are younger. Older customers generally desire more "human touch"—personal interaction and conversation—than younger customers, who crave speed and efficiency, as well as digital information at the touch of a button. The same is true for various cultures; Hispanics often have a more social and personal approach to the purchase process and will engage a sales associate in a discussion unrelated to the product or service being sold. Many immigrants, especially those who've recently arrived in the United States, may have more questions about a product. They appreciate it when a salesperson gives them all the time that they need to talk and ask questions. Even men tend to want different things than women do: whereas males prefer to have choices narrowed and simplified, women generally like to look at numerous options.

All of these different types of customer needs, wants, and expectations put additional pressure on your employees. They not only need to be good employees in all the basic ways—polite, responsive, helpful, and knowledgeable—but also need to be flexible, adaptable, and culturally sensitive. And they can't be intimidated by the prospect of assisting someone who is not like them.

That's a tall order. You probably know how hard it is to find good people in the first place. I can just hear the voice in your head: "Wow. I want smart, talented employees who have a good work ethic, who are customer-focused, honest, and ethical. And it would be ideal if they have good judgment and are resourceful, too. And now you want to add that they need to be culturally aware and highly adaptable *too?* C'mon! That's *impossible!*"

It's not impossible. In fact, it's necessary. You were smart enough to pick up this book in the first place, and you've read the first six chapters. You clearly understand how important the customer experience is today, and you know it's not a one-size-fits-all world anymore. How can the piece of the puzzle that involves your employees not be the most important piece of all? They are the ones who will, to a great extent, actually embody the experience. They are the ones who will be remembered, either in a positive light or a negative one. They are the ones who will meet your prospects' need, solve their problems, and keep them coming back for more—*or not.*

Your employees are the ones who will be remembered. They're the ones who will meet your customers' needs, solve their problems, and keep them coming back—*or not.*

I am not suggesting that it's *easy* to find, train, and develop employees like this. But your ability to deliver a great customer experience for people not like you depends even more on your frontline employees. They need to be sensitive to the nuances of what different customers want and need. *It's not easy.* If it were, everyone would be doing it, including your competition. But since no one really *is*, you've got a great opportunity to shine and develop a significant competitive edge.

So how do you get your employees to embrace—and deliver—a customer experience that makes different types of people feel valued and makes them do business with you over and over again?

There are several things you can do to make sure you get this right.

FIRST THINGS FIRST: HIRE THE RIGHT PERSON

It all starts with the right hiring decisions. Most of us try to find people who have a particular skill set for the positions we have open, which is important much of the time—but not always. Sometimes, you have a position available at your company with *teachable* job duties. When you have such positions open, focus on the *kind of person* you want to hire; don't worry about whether the applicant has previous experience in a similar capacity.

I realize that this is not always going to be possible. After all, if you need a skilled technician at your body shop, then that's what you need. But many jobs are composed of teachable, trainable tasks, and these types of positions allow you to focus on the applicant's attitude and ability to empathize. You can do that by creating open-ended dialogue that draws the candidate out, such as, "Describe the approach you'd take in working with a new customer (or someone who just walked into the store). How would you determine the best way to help him or her?" That kind of revealing conversation lets you maneuver to ask more probing questions, such as, "How would you modify that approach if the customer were speaking another language?" (or "if the customer was older?" "of a different race or ethnicity?" or "a mom with two kids?")

When talking with potential employees, *you're looking for their ability to put themselves in the customer's shoes.*

You're looking for potential hires' ability to put themselves in someone else's shoes.

Bill Thompson is the "Guru of Customer Happiness" at olark.com, a software company that specializes in live chat (customer service). Olark.com hires people who *fit their culture of empathy.* Following are the six personality characteristics that Thompson's company looks for in new hires. These are the traits that will best serve your customers, especially those who are not like you:

1. **Genuine warmth:** A person who exudes friendliness, caring about other people, and an upbeat and outgoing personality.
2. **Empathic:** Someone who is able to understand other people's feelings and relate well and be sympathetic to someone under stress.

3. **A good listener:** A person who listens actively in order to fully understand an issue or problem before acting.
4. **Conscientious:** It sounds basic, but it's vital to have people who naturally take pride in taking care of every little detail perfectly.
5. **Anticipatory:** Although this sounds as though it's antithetical to #3, it's slightly different. People who are excellent at anticipating cause and effect can save a great deal of time. They don't just answer the question at hand but also dig deep to make sure they've resolved every aspect of the customer's problem by the time the conversation is over.
6. **Optimistic:** Again, it sounds basic, but an optimistic attitude is vital in avoiding burnout. The daily exposure to people who are occasionally stressed out—and not always the friendliest—can drag a person down.

If you find these characteristics in an applicant, *hire him or her!* That individual has the personality foundation to be trained and developed to deliver great customer service to anyone, even people who are different.

NEXT: INSTILL A CULTURE THAT VALUES DIVERSITY

Great employees will adopt—and enforce—your culture. Every business has a culture, and no matter what other values comprise your company's culture, valuing and respecting *diversity* should be one of them. This doesn't simply require that you respect different races, ethnicities, and religions. *Diversity of thought* is important as well. A culture that values and respects diversity will support the notion that there is more than one way to do things. Your employees need to know that they can have diverse opinions, perspectives, experiences, and impressions. None of these are right or wrong, as long as they're meeting customers' needs, exceeding their expectations, and achieving the company's goals in the process.

You may be lucky enough to have employees who "get" diversity of thought and experience, but chances are, you'll need to set the tone and your expectations. They need to hear—from you—why diversity is a business opportunity and how you can grow the company by serving a broad, diverse group of customers. Once you've established that your organization not only values but *desires* diverse customer groups, you can start training your team on how to handle these different groups' needs and wants.

NEXT: EMPLOYEE TRAINING

You want to engage the employees themselves as much as possible when you are training your employees on how to deliver a terrific customer experience for diverse customer segments. Hold ongoing meetings where you pose hypothetical questions about what it would be like for someone who is different from them to try to do business with you. For example, "If a 65-year-old, retired customer came in or called, what would you do to make that person comfortable doing business with us? What might that customer want from us, *besides* our product/service?" You can then ask how that customer's needs and wants might differ from someone who is four decades younger. For example, if you ask your employees what they'd do if someone came in who didn't speak their language, hopefully one of the first responses you'd hear from your team would be, "I'd smile at him or her and say hello." The *smile* part is the important part, because a smile sends the message that "Even though there is a language barrier, I am glad you're here and I'll try to help you." This type of conversation with your staff will generate great ideas and identify potential barriers you must overcome in serving customers effectively.

Here's a different example. Let's say that you posed a question to your staff about a different hypothetical customer: a mom with a tired, cranky toddler. An employee might suggest greeting the mom first, then saying hello to the child and giving him or her a lollipop, a balloon, or a coloring book and crayons. Just think how grateful a frazzled mom would be to have her child blissfully occupied while she talked with your employee.

There are lots of diversity training programs available online and hundreds of articles on dos and don'ts. You don't necessarily have to hire an outside training company to teach your staff how to work with diverse groups. That's certainly an option, but such a critical part of making people feel valued and appreciated is simply common sense and paying attention to the customer's needs in the first place.

I know that you're busy. Every successful businessperson out there is completely slammed. Their schedules are jam-packed, and they work long hours and juggle a million tasks. You may be asking yourself, in light of the amount of pressure you're under, "How am I going to find the time to train my staff like this?" Although you probably agree philosophically with the value of training, allocating the time may seem daunting. I get it.

But ask yourself, "What's the value of having a well-trained employee who not only is focused on providing customer delight but also is able to actually *deliver that* to different customer groups? What would I have to spend in terms of advertising and marketing to draw new customers in and keep them?" That's the amount you should be allocating to staffing and training your people properly—whether you spend actual dollars on training or whether it's the cost of your time to do so and continually reinforce its importance. You can "invest" those marketing dollars in your people; they will deliver more bang for your buck than any advertising will.

IMPORTANT: BE ATTUNED TO SUBTLETIES

When you're teaching your staff to pay attention to customers' needs, emphasize that they not only need to listen to what customers say but must also watch their faces and mannerisms. An example of a brand that does this extremely well is Disney. Not only are they the world's most powerful entertainment brand, but they're also known for the incredible customer experience they provide. When you think about it, it's astonishing that the millions and millions of people who go to Disney World each year virtually *all* have a positive—if not delightful—experience. How is that possible? How can Disney make so many different people, *from all over the world*, happy?

It's because Disney sees themselves not just in the entertainment business but in the "business of making magical memories." To do this, they train their people to anticipate visitors' problems and issues. When staff members (called cast members) see a guest with a puzzled expression on his or her face, they proactively approach the person and ask if there is something they can help with. *They don't wait for the guest to come to them.*

You can do the same thing with your team: teach them to look for body language and facial expressions that will cue them as to how they might be able to best help a specific customer. Let me give you an example:

Breanna Ridge is my barista at my local Starbucks, and she is fantastic. She is friendly, is outgoing, and provides incredibly fast service. But more important than that, she's highly attuned to her customers' needs. Sure, they are all there to get a coffee beverage from her, but the *way* that they need service from her can vary extensively. Breanna said the following about delivering a great customer experience to diverse people: "I see it all the time. I've got a guy who comes in every day who talks on his phone the whole time and just points at the menu board for what he wants. At first, I thought he was kind of rude. But I came to realize that he makes business calls on his way to work, and that's when he's coming in to get his coffee. He's all about multitasking because he doesn't have much time. So now when he comes in, I smile at him and point to the menu board and he smiles back and nods and I can make his drink. He doesn't have to stop his business conversation. I make his beverage and ring him up and we never actually speak. But I am giving him what he wants—efficient, fast service, with no interruptions. He comes in every day and is one of my best customers."

Breanna went on to tell me that using this same approach with another of her regulars would backfire. She has another customer who is an older woman who lives alone. She's very lonely and wants someone to talk to. She's retired, so she's never in a rush to get her coffee quickly and move on. In fact, Breanna says, the woman sometimes stays for 2 hours, chatting with Breanna between customers. This customer doesn't just want a cup of coffee; she wants *companionship*, someone to visit with. Breanna understands this and gives this customer as much attention as she can while she works and waits on other customers as well.

These differences are subtle. But you can tell a great deal about someone by paying attention to mannerisms, body language, and expressions—whether they are comfortable or not, stressed, confused, or overwhelmed. Teach your employees the importance of focusing on the whole person, not just the words they say.

BE GRACIOUS—*NO MATTER WHAT*

I was a keynote speaker recently for a company called Halloween Express, the parent company for franchisees with seasonal, temporary stores that sell Halloween costumes and supplies. At their conference, I spoke with a sales associate who told me a story of assisting a very overweight customer, a woman who wanted to wear a Spiderman costume to a party. Halloween Express had the costume in stock and the woman went into the dressing room to try it on. The sales associate stood outside the dressing room, ready to assist with anything the customer might need. When she asked her how she was doing and if she liked the costume, the customer came out, stood before the mirror, and said sadly, "I look terrible." The Spiderman costume is a very tight, very formfitting, and very unforgiving costume. It shows every little ripple and bulge on even the thinnest of wearers. It didn't look very good on this large woman, and she knew it. Her expression told the sales associate that not only was the customer disappointed; she was also embarrassed.

The salesperson asked her, "Have you thought about being a Geisha instead? If you're going to be at a party all night, the Geisha costume is so much more comfortable than the Spiderman one." She got the costume, which was a large, flowy Japanese robe. The customer tried it on and was thrilled! She looked—and felt—much better. She bought the entire Geisha ensemble: robe, shoes, face makeup, chopsticks, wig, and more. And the sale was significantly higher than if she'd just purchased the Spiderman costume.

But what impressed me more was the sales associate's graciousness. She provided a solution to the customer by way of a different costume, but she framed it as "This is more comfortable," *not* "This will look better." By positioning it like that, she didn't embarrass the woman or make her feel self-conscious. She gave her a solution that preserved her dignity. Best of all, that same woman comes back year after year to get her costumes from that store. Although she has countless options for purchasing a Halloween costume—Walmart, Target, costume rental shops—Halloween Express earned this customer's business for years, simply by being gracious.

Stories like this really highlight the importance of your frontline employees and emphasize the fact that they can make or break your business.

Delivering an exceptional experience for diverse customers depends even *more* on your frontline employees. Stay focused on the four things you must do to ensure that your employees are positioned to fulfill that goal:

1. **Make the right hires.** Look for people who share your passion for great customer service and hire them. You can always teach them your business, but you can't teach someone how to empathize and put the customer first.
2. **Train them on the importance of catering to diverse customer segments.** Actively engage them in conversations and role-playing with different scenarios.
3. **Be attuned to nuances.** Mannerisms, expressions, and attitude can be clues to what customers really need from you, whether they voice it or not.
4. **Be gracious.** No matter what. Don't ever laugh at customers, embarrass them, or humiliate them. Be kind and solution-oriented, and you will win their loyalty.

CHAPTER 8

Seven Principles for Creating a Customer Experience for People Not Like You

This part of the book focuses on crafting the customer experience for specific groups of people—members of different generations, members of different races/ethnicities, women, families, gays and lesbians, and more. But before we tackle this, it's important to take a look at all the different customer touch points, since the customer experience doesn't just happen when someone buys something. A customer's experience is shaped by the *entire interaction* with your brand, product, service, or company—from beginning to end.

The following sections discuss the seven principles to crafting a customer experience for people not like you.

1. WEBSITE/DIGITAL COMMUNICATION

Most people will initially find you online or will visit your website or Facebook page to check you out if they heard about you via word of mouth. You want to make sure that your website and your social media pages are welcoming to diverse groups. The least you can do is feature people who don't all look the same if you use pictures of people on your site or pages. Find imagery that shows different races, ages, even lifestyle cues such as dress, tattoos, or braids. People always want to identify with someone who looks like them, so be certain that you display a range of representation when it comes to showing people. If you want to really put the welcome mat out for a *particular* customer group, flag them with a question or callout on your page. For example, famous fruit and vegetable producer Dole's website home page doesn't list all the products and produce they sell. Instead, they feature *nutrition*. They have tabs for eating right (with information on fruits, vegetables, juices, and salads, as well as recipes) and living right (including fitness tips and weight loss tips). But they also have a tab called SuperKids that's prominently positioned at the top of the their page. Although kids can certainly access this

FIGURE 8.1 Dole targets moms with the promise of "SuperKids."

section—which features games, music, comics, videos, and more—I can guarantee that the customer group they're trying to attract and engage with this is *moms*. Dole knows that the way to a mom's heart is through her child. They could have called the section "Moms," but by labeling it SuperKids and providing content that moms care about, such as tasty, nutritious recipes and fun fitness ideas, they are reaching moms *first*, and then their kids. What mom doesn't want her kid to be a SuperKid? And what kid doesn't want to be one? It's brilliant. Figure 8.1 is a screen shot from the brand's website home page.

This type of "welcome mat" doesn't just have to occur on your website; Facebook pages can have similarly customized tabs. Figure 8.2 is a screen shot from the Dole Facebook page. You can see their customized tabs.

Your website is also a great way to cater to a group who speaks another language. You can let them know this by clearly posting these other language(s) at the top of the page in which a customer can navigate. If it's too costly to develop an entirely separate website in another language, a smart alternative is to create a page that has the most frequently asked questions or most sought-after information. You have to create only one or two pages in another language with this approach; it's a cost-effective way to let customers and prospects know that you understand they may prefer to navigate your site in their native tongue. And don't hide it if you *do* have a website in

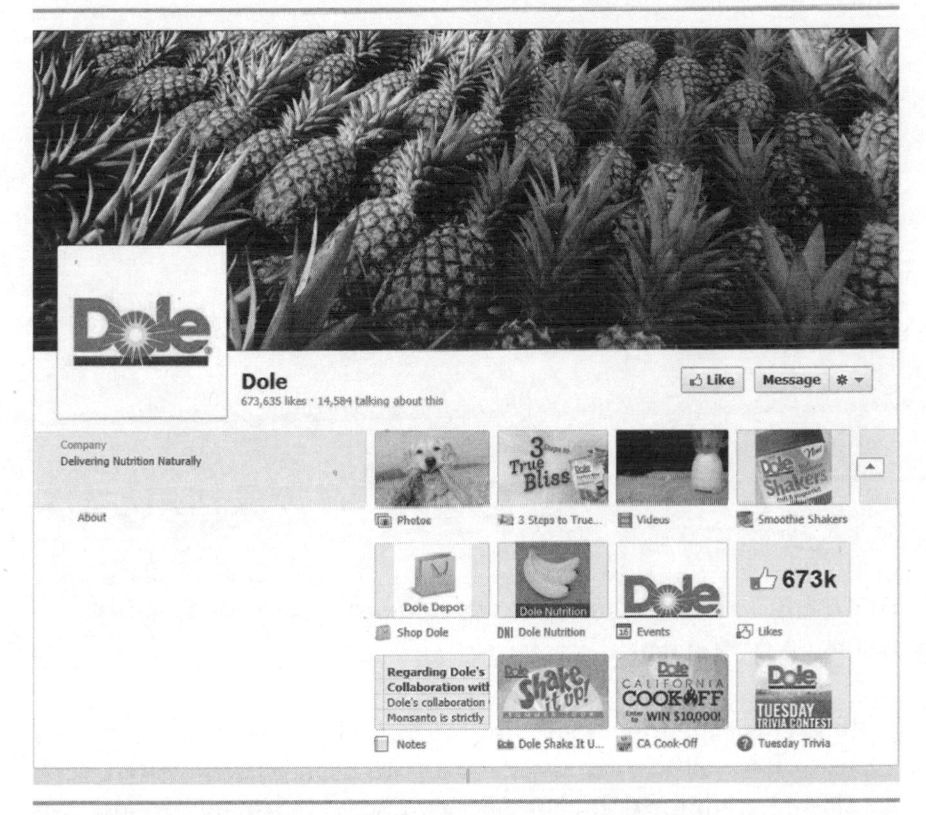

FIGURE 8.2 Dole uses customized Facebook tabs to convey different information to different types of customers.

another language; feature it prominently! I love the home page for Lowe's hardware stores (Figure 8.3); the Spanish option is first at the top, even before the Help tab or their weekly specials. By prominently showcasing a site in Spanish, Lowe's starts the customer experience off on the right foot for an entire segment of customers.

2. PRODUCT OR SERVICE TWEAKS

To reach people not like you—or not like the customers you already have—sometimes you need to tweak your product or service. Modifying a product or service in this way can mean a great deal to someone of a specific market segment. It can be a small change,

FIGURE 8.3 Lowe's "puts the welcome mat" out for Spanish-speaking customers.

such as creating an iPad app for your business that tech-savvy Gen Y customers will want to use, or it can be a bit more involved, such as adding traditional Indian, Vietnamese, or Hispanic foods to a menu. It can also be a big alteration; for example, perhaps you create an entirely new product to serve someone different from your core customers.

For example, a new casino resort called Revel recently opened in Atlantic City. You might be wondering, "What's so special about a new casino resort in Atlantic City, the largest gambling mecca in the United States outside of Las Vegas?" After all, the city is home to dozens of casino resorts. But what makes Revel unique is that it is the only one in Atlantic City that is a *nonsmoking* casino resort—and you know how unusual this is if you've ever been to a casino. Casinos are typically thick with smoke. But Revel was created for the 81 percent of Americans who *don't* smoke, which is an incredibly smart idea. The developers obviously knew that there is an entire (and large!) segment of the population who might like to gamble but are turned off by smoky casinos because they're nonsmokers—and therefore they just don't go. Until now, that is.

Revel offers nonsmokers a place to play and have fun while breathing clean air. Now that's a *big* tweak, creating a casino for a specific customer group and perhaps losing some business from people who prefer to smoke while they gamble. However, it shows that you can succeed and grow business when you reach out to a new customer group with a product or service that is relevant to them.

3. HIRING AND STAFFING DIVERSE TALENT

I wrote extensively about this key point in the last chapter, because it is truly your single *best tactic* for creating a fantastic customer experience for people not like you. Who knows better than a Gen Y person what another Gen Y person may want, need, or value? Who better than a retired person to connect with others who are also older and/or retired? An African American sales associate or female sales associate may be able to interact more successfully with other African Americans or women than anyone else on your staff. An Asian employee may have unique insights into the local Asian community that you simply don't have. A bilingual employee who speaks Spanish as well as English will be a huge asset, because he or she is likely to understand the *culture*, not just the language. When you hire people who are not like you, you'll see your business grow with new customers very quickly. That's because we all have a network of friends, neighbors, and family—people we tell about where we work and what we do. So when you hire someone who is tapped into a whole new network, word will get around that your place of business is the place to go. Then when you treat these new customers with respect, care, and understanding, you show that you value them. And assuming they like whatever it is that you sell or provide, they'll stay with you and become loyal repeat customers.

4. ADVERTISING AND MARKETING

Once you have a diverse team in place—or even just one person on your staff who is different from you—you can effectively advertise and market to that new customer group or groups. Although this may seem obvious, you'd be surprised how many times business owners ask me if they can advertise to the Hispanic market in their community if they don't have anyone on staff who speaks Spanish. The answer is *no!* I understand that they've read all the news articles about the growth of the Hispanic market and are eager to grow their business with new customers. But you can't market to a new and different customer group, at least, not authentically, if there is no one on board who represents that customer. For example, there is a yoga studio directly across the street from my house. They post their class schedule, complete with type of class, time, and instructor name, on their window. Just from observation, I'd guess that 90 to 95 percent of the people who take classes there are young women, in their 20s and early 30s. I never used to see any men of *any* age go there. Then one day, I was walking by and looked at their schedule posted in the window; prominently featured was "Introducing New Ashram Yoga Class with Yogi David Fordham! Beginners Welcome!" Not only were they clearly promoting that the instructor was a man, they also made it obvious that even if you've never taken a yoga class before, you would not feel out of place in this class. It was such a smart thing to do; chances are, if you're not getting many men in your yoga classes, then the ones who might now come are almost certainly going to be beginners. I know the studio owners, and they told me that 25 percent of their students/attendees are now men, up from less than 5 percent just a year ago. Having a male instructor makes other men feel comfortable. They don't feel out of place, like they're the only guy in the class. When you hire and staff with diverse talent, you'll see your business grow with new faces.

5. STAFF INTERACTIONS

Train. Monitor. Coach. Reinforce. That's the mantra. First you have to train your great employees to actively engage with diverse customers in a meaningful way. But you also need to monitor them to ensure that they are on the right track. Listen in on their conversations with customers, observe how they work with diverse people, and pay attention to customers' reactions. If you've got someone who is performing well in this regard, then praise him or her. Let that person know that you have noticed how well he or she is doing and that you appreciate the efforts. If someone is not performing up to your standards, provide coaching on what can be done better. Tell this employee, as specifically as you can, how he or she could improve or how to work with a customer more effectively. Then give that person a chance to demonstrate that he or she can adapt and do better. Continue monitoring, observing, and coaching until the customer approach becomes a habit or second nature. And continually reinforce the importance of crafting unique customer experiences for diverse customers. Keep your team abreast of how their efforts are paying off. Perhaps even share sales results with them as appropriate, for example, "Since we've begun our training efforts and new customer approach, our sales are up 15 percent over last quarter." Or praise the exceptional way that a particular employee handled a specific customer situation. For example, "Kudos to Bob for the way he helped our new customer from Venezuela last week. The customer was unfamiliar with the U.S. sizing standards and didn't know his size, so Bob spent time working with him to determine his correct size, then pulled all the merchandise in that size that the customer was interested in. In fact, the customer came in looking for a jersey, but also bought two pair of cleats, socks, and other accessories. Great job, Bob." When you review positive examples like this with your staff—in the kind of detail used here—you accomplish two important things:

1. You recognize an employee's efforts and publicly praise that person for a job well done. (And as a side note, what does this cost you? Nothing! Praise is free. And the best part is that even though it costs nothing, it can mean *everything* to the employee receiving it. We all appreciate recognition.)
2. It teaches other staff members what to do and how they can handle a similar situation. It sets the bar. It also continually reinforces that this is not just some "initiative flavor of the month" but that you care about this, that you're paying attention to it on an ongoing basis, and that it is a company priority.

6. CUSTOMER SERVICE AND SUPPORT

We all expect that a company will stand by its products or services. But you can enhance the customer experience for people not like you by thinking through all aspects of what it's like to do business with you, for people of all backgrounds and situations. For instance, one of my friends is a divorced father of two young girls. He is an active, involved dad, completely committed to effectively coparenting his daughters. He told me recently about a problem he was having with all of their after-school activities, which include swimming lessons, soccer, and a dance class for the oldest. Since my friend has part-time custody of his girls, he finds himself taking them to their classes when they are staying with him. The problem is that the girls' mother is the only one who receives e-mails and updates about all the classes and activities! Their dad is totally in the dark if a class is canceled or rescheduled due to weather, and so on. He and his ex-wife finally figured out a way to keep him in the loop, simply by putting an automatic "forward" function on all the e-mails the mom receives.

However, this dad is outraged. He can't believe, in this day and age—when so many families share custody of children or have blended families—that these organizations haven't set up something as important as e-mail communication to handle more than one e-mail address per child! Many after-school activities do make sure both parents are in the communication loop, but in this man's case, he found it infuriating (and rightfully so!) that *all* of his daughters' activities shared the same issue. I'm betting that the minute a viable alternative dance class or a different place to swim comes along that offers a more robust *parental* (not just for moms) communication system, this dad will take his business there.

Another example of great customer support for different groups is one for a public storage facility near a military base. They have three types of customers: people who simply have too much stuff and would rather store it than sell it, young people who have lost a job or a home and have had to move back in with their parents temporarily, and members of the military who are being deployed and need to store some or all of their belongings. This storage facility realized that the *payment needs* of their various customers are very different. Their military customers want to set everything up to be paid automatically from their checking accounts once a month. It's clean, easy, and automatic—and one less thing for someone overseas to worry about. But the young, financially struggling individuals may find it difficult to make a payment once a month. It may be easier for them to come up with $15 each week than $60 all at once at the beginning of the month. So the storage facility created different ways that customers can pay. This is a great example of ongoing customer service and support to different types of people. Both groups need storage. It's the way they prefer to *pay* for this that differs. And if you were in either of those customer groups, wouldn't you appreciate that someone knows and understands your situation and makes it easier for you to purchase their service because of it?

7. AFTER THE SALE

Of course, the customer experience doesn't end after you've made the sale (see Figure 8.4). Even though the purchase may be complete, the "ownership" experience is just beginning. Remember the purchase funnel from Chapter 3? After the purchase comes loyalty and finally (hopefully), advocacy. To become—and remain—loyal to your product or service, the customer has to continue to have a great experience. Part of that is how your product or service performs, of course. But the other part is what the ongoing experience is like for your customer. I recently read an interesting article that drove this point home for me. It was about how airports are trying to cater to business travelers even

FIGURE 8.4 The purchase funnel doesn't end with a customer's purchase. The last–and best—stage is "advocacy."

more by adding workout facilities within the airport. Think about it: if you are in an airport, either flying to or from it or connecting through, *you are already their customer.* You're there. But airports want you to keep coming back. They want you to fly out of their airport in areas where you may have a choice among others. By offering a workout facility at a nominal charge, they are providing a valuable benefit to business travelers who fly frequently and may find it very difficult to maintain their fitness routine on the road. And what better way to spend a 2-hour weather delay than by getting a good workout in? It's an amenity that some airports are offering *after the sale* to show a specific customer group (in this case, frequent business travelers) that they understand them (how tough it is to be a road warrior) and that they are trying to make their travel easier or better in any way that they can.

In the next few chapters, we'll dive into some key customer groups that can help grow your business. The seven principles outlined here apply in all cases. Use this list as your guide and your checklist to think through all the customer touch points for your business when you're cultivating customers who are not like you.

CHAPTER 9

Matures, Boomers, Gen X, Gen Y, and Gen Z

We established in the first part of this book that the customer experience is, without a doubt, one that you can uniquely shape for a number of different high-potential market segments. Businesses are no longer one size fits all, and never will be again. Perhaps nowhere is this more evident than in comparing different generations' customer experience wants, needs, and expectations.

I love talking about generational differences, because everyone can relate to them. After all, not everyone has the experience of being a member of a different cultural, racial, or ethnic group, nor has everyone undergone lifestyle/life change differences like being a mom or having a family. But everyone has an age. And everyone knows, loves, works with, or sells to someone who is of a different generation.

A great deal has been written about the different generations' work styles. But I find that there's a void of good information and advice out there about understanding what people want from you and your business. This chapter will cover how you can craft a terrific customer experience for the five generations that are currently in the marketplace. The following are the five generations and the approximate years of birth that define each. Depending on whose research you read, the years may vary a bit, but these represent a good guideline for understanding the general definition of each generation:

Matures	Born before 1946
Baby boomers	Born 1946–1964
Gen X	Born 1965–1981
Gen Y	Born 1982–2004
Gen Z	2005–present

My caveat for this chapter, as well as the subsequent chapters, is that it's obviously impossible to lump all people of a particular group into a category and say, "These people are like *this.*" And it doesn't matter whether we're referring to a group by gender, age, race, ethnicity, or income. Such broad generalizations are inherently stereotypical and clearly won't apply to every single member of a particular group. But there are often shared experiences, which lead to shared values, among people of a certain group. It is with this view that I offer the following general characteristics of the generations, their perspectives, and what they respond to best when it comes to their customer experience and satisfaction.

MATURES

Called the mature generation or sometimes "traditionalists," this is the oldest generation living today. They were profoundly shaped by experiences such as the Great Depression, World War II, and the Korean War. They tend to hold traditional values of duty: to God, to country, to neighbor, to community, and to friend. They believe in being a team player and pulling their own weight. Computers didn't enter the picture until they were well into their careers, if they had a career at all; women of this generation often did not work outside the home and were full-time homemakers, wives, and mothers. Therefore, they have been slower to adapt to technology. They also were not nearly as exposed as subsequent generations to *people not like themselves.* For this generation, segregation in schools was a fact of life, and communities in which they lived reflected that same segregation. Whites did not necessarily go to school with blacks or even live in the same parts of town. Racial and ethnic groups kept to their own communities, and minorities in the workforce were not typically members of management. Most were in lower and mid-level positions.

This generation has seen a lot of cultural change over their lifetime, often change that rocked their world. They witnessed desegregation of schools and communities in the 1950s and 1960s and women entering the workforce in huge numbers in the 1970s. They've seen interracial marriages declared legal, antidiscrimination laws enacted, and people being openly gay in their communities. They've seen families move away from each other to different parts of the country; many have grandchildren who communicate with them only via texting.

This generation has been through huge societal shifts, and sometimes they wonder where the world as they knew it has gone.

This means you need to emphasize personal connection and focus on humanness when crafting a customer service experience for matures—and not just focus on their wallets. These people grew up in an era when everyone knew their neighbors, and you could rely on people for help, advice, and companionship. Our world today is much different. We often don't know our neighbors at all. We rely on the Internet, articles, and information to give us answers, rather than relying on conversation with others. And we connect with others online for companionship and a sense of community. So when it comes to delighting this generation's customers, keep in mind and focus on the following three things:

1. **High touch is more important than high tech.** Members of this group value speed and efficiency much less than they do being treated as individuals.
2. **Socializing face-to-face is crucial.** Be ready to connect with them, perhaps by sharing a personal story—and asking about their own.
3. **Delivering service at particular times of day may need to vary.** Matures may want and appreciate earlier business hours than other customer groups.

High Touch over High Tech

Although many members of this generation *are* very tech-savvy, *many are not*—and even those who are still highly value *connecting with other people.* It's how they were socialized. Therefore, despite the fact that technology may make many transactions and sales faster, easier, and more efficient, this generation would frequently prefer to forego the tech tools that appeal to others and opt instead for a human interaction.

Let me give you an example. I fly every week and almost every day. I am a huge fan of the self-service kiosks at the airports; they allow me to check in and get my boarding pass in about 60 seconds or less. And almost every time I fly, I see kiosks that are available for use—yet a long line of people are still standing in line, waiting to talk to a ticket agent. I can understand wanting to talk with someone if you have to change your ticket or have other complicating travel issues. But I have found by eavesdropping on many of these customers' transactions that they are simply checking in for their flight just as I am. And I've also found that the age of the average person standing in this line is typically older, usually a member of the mature generation. Despite the tech tool (kiosks) that can speed up the check-in process for them, they'll stand in line, sometimes for 10 to 15 minutes, just to conduct the process with a living human being. This makes sense for two reasons: First, They may be less comfortable or knowledgeable about how the kiosks work and the potential for confusion isn't worth the added stress to them. They may not have confidence in the automated procedure. (I see this constantly when people are asked to insert a credit card to identify themselves; they are afraid they will be charged for their ticket a second time.) Second, *They prefer to talk with someone.* It's that simple. If you're checking me in for my flight, I can say hello, ask you any other questions I may have, and feel a general sense of confidence that I am in the right place and doing the right thing—because a human being has assured me as much. A smile, a pleasant word, perhaps some quick chat about where the traveler is headed makes it a more personal, enjoyable experience, even if that experience takes longer. That high touch encounter likely trumps a fast, efficient machine transaction every time.

Socializing Face-to-Face Is Very Important

Again, because this generation was raised knowing their friends, neighbors, and community members personally, they are most comfortable with talking face-to-face. They don't mind making time for others, and they expect others to make time for them. And it's a growing challenge in our ever-speeded-up world to make time for each other and for *live* (not digital) conversation. But this generation really appreciates interacting with others face-to-face and sharing their lives and personal stories with others. So if you want to craft an exceptional customer experience for a mature, you must evaluate the aspects of your business that can foster this kind of social interaction.

A bank in Saint Petersburg, Florida, did just that. The majority of their clientele is matures. Rather than have customers wait in an impersonal line to talk with a teller, they eliminated the lines altogether and installed a living room–like area with couches, chairs, and end tables in which their customers can wait. This warm atmosphere promotes visiting among the customers, who swap stories and pass the time by talking with one another. They even make new friends this way. Suddenly, the bank isn't just a place to go and make a deposit or get cash. Now it's a fun place to visit where customers can talk with one another while taking care of their personal business.

I was speaking at a chiropractic conference last year and met a young chiropractor whose practice is in Arizona. Like Florida, Arizona has a huge retiree and mature population. About 30 percent of his patients were matures. Many of them have a lot of time on their hands and are often lonely for someone to talk to, so having an appointment with him is a big part of their day. They look forward to and enjoy talking with the doctor, and in addition to discussing their aches and pains, they like sharing their stories of their grandchildren and other personal stories.

However, this clearly puts a great deal of customer service pressure on the young chiropractor. He needs to see a lot of patients on any given day, which he can do only if he stays on schedule. He allocates a certain amount of time for each patient's care and consultation. It doesn't take much chitchat for him to fall behind on his schedule, yet he understands how important that aspect of the patient experience is to his customers. They don't want to be hustled in and out of his office. They want to visit and talk and are in no hurry, even though he is. So he came up with a fantastic solution.

When one of his mature patients would start to talk extensively about matters beyond his or her physical care, he'd say, "Mrs. [or Mr.] Johnson, I want to hear all about your visit to your daughter's home. But I have lots of patients to see, and I want to be able to give you my undivided attention. Why don't you come to my Donuts with the Doctor breakfast on Tuesday? It's from 7 AM to 9 AM, it's free—and I provide donuts and coffee for anyone who wants to drop by. I don't take any patient exams during that time. It's a special 2-hour time period where I can really catch up with you and my other patients in a way that I can't do on most days. How does that sound? Will you please come?"

This is a brilliant idea. It satisfies his mature customers in so many ways: it makes them feel special and important ("I want to hear all about your vacation, grandkids, etc."), it invites them to something fun and extra in their lives (a complimentary breakfast), and it gives the doctor a graceful, diplomatic way to manage his time without having to tell a patient, "Not now. I'm busy." It's such a simple idea, and one that costs the doctor nothing more than the price of some donuts and coffee each week. He normally doesn't see patients until 9 AM anyway, so he hasn't even cut into his patient schedule by holding Donuts with the Doctor from 7 AM to 9 AM.

When I asked him how it was working, he told me, "It's the best thing I've ever done. When I started it, 30 percent of my patients were older or elderly. Now, more than 50 percent are. And not only am I getting new patients from their referrals all the time, but they won't go anywhere else. They love coming to see me, even for the smallest thing." Now *that's* a success story—all because this chiropractor was smart enough to realize what his mature customers want.

Delivering Service at Particular Times of Day May Need to Vary

Most people who make plans to go out to eat and hear a live band think about eating mid-evening and watching live entertainment that usually starts later, around 10 PM or so. But for many matures, live entertainment that starts at 10 PM simply doesn't work. As you get older, you tend to awaken earlier in the day—but also get sleepy earlier in the evening. That's why so many restaurants in areas with lots of matures have "sunset dinners," meals served from 4:30 PM until 6:30 PM. It's a way for a restaurant to bring in customers before the normal dinner rush and satisfy their older customers, who want to be home before dark.

A lot of these same restaurants have realized that just because someone is mature doesn't mean he or she doesn't want to listen to live music. So many restaurants in Sarasota, Florida, cater to matures by having live entertainment from 6 PM to 10 PM. The band is packing up and heading home at a time when most bands are usually just getting started.

Little tweaks like this to your customer service can mean everything to mature customers. And if you show them that you care about what they want, they will reward you with their repeat business.

BABY BOOMERS

The boomers are the "me" generation. Self-absorbed, self-aware, and self-sufficient, they grew up with definite ideas about what is good for them and the country. They are more knowledgeable, educated, and affluent than any other generation before them has been. They have a youthful mind-set and refuse to grow old. They value experiences. Most of all, they value how they see themselves—and that's how they want you to see them, too.

Here are the key principles to keep in mind when providing a great customer experience for baby boomers:

- **They desire personal growth.** Whether it's becoming fitter, learning another language, or seeing polar bears in their natural habitat, boomers want to do it—and be able *to tell others* that they did it. They feel a need to have a cause and visit places, species, and lifestyles that are vanishing to experience them for themselves. If you can show boomers how your product or service fits into their personal growth—and reflects well on them—you'll be tapping right into what they value most.
- **They value professionals.** Previous generations placed much more value on self-reliance and doing things themselves, whether it was mowing the lawn or doing their own financial planning. Boomers, on the other hand, are fine with letting the experts, whether it's their broker, their decorator, their landscaper, or their nutritionist, take care of them. When you are dealing with baby boomers, showcase how the product or service you offer fits in with their desire for individual attention. A good example of this is the local gym. Most gyms have lots of classes for members, which offer the most affordable way to take advantage of a membership. But gyms learned early on that many boomers don't want to be part of the "masses" by taking the same class that everyone else is taking. They want individual attention and are willing to pay for it. So, in addition to the equipment and classes that gyms offer, they also offer individual sessions with personal trainers, yoga instructors, and Pilates instructors. Boomers want to feel special, and having their "own, dedicated professional," even for just an hour at a time, is preferable to feeling like just one of the group.

- **They desire to be self-sufficient.** Boomers are independent thinkers who often pride themselves on being nonconformists. They want their adventurous spirit, openness to trying new things, and progressive views on the world to help them stand out from others (in a good way). But to be truly self-sufficient, they must be informed—and not made vulnerable. Therefore, you must remove risk as much as you can to provide a great customer experience for boomers. Teach them what they need to know, logically, emotionally, and thoroughly. Give them all the information they need to make an informed decision. Then let them decide.

  We can see a clear example of this in the travel and tourism industry. Boomers are very, very different travelers than previous generations. Travel tours for matures typically focus on keeping the travelers comfortable in their surroundings. Many matures want to avoid any hassles with other countries' languages, currencies, unfamiliar foods, and lodging. Travel companies provide them with English-speaking tour operators, preplanned itineraries that take care of every detail, and familiar-looking food, utensils, and environments.

  For boomers, however, the better customer experience is *one of their own making*. Boomers want extensive information on everything there is to see and do, and then the freedom to explore on their own. They don't necessarily want to see landmarks and interesting sites as part of a tour group. They are comfortable striking out on their own and exploring, as long as they feel informed and knowledgeable. Therefore, the best customer experience that the travel tourism business can provide is one in which customers build their own tour, with numerous options and built-in free time for boomers to choose their own activities.
- **Their kids and pets are the center of the universe.** Because the boomers themselves feel special, it follows that their kids and pets are special, too. But since most boomers have older or grown children now, their focus has shifted to their pets. Catering to their pets has proved to be highly lucrative for businesses. For instance, there are a lot of upscale bars and restaurants in my downtown Dallas neighborhood, including one small, intimate place nearby called the Alcove. It's a quiet little spot that hosts wine tastings and draws an affluent crowd. They offer both indoor and outdoor

seating. In addition to the wine tasting events that they have, they always have water bowls and free dog biscuits for their patrons' dogs. Baby boomers in the neighborhood walk their dogs and will stop by for a drink. They sit outside and enjoy a glass of wine while Fido gets a dog biscuit and a drink of water. What a great way to turn passersby into customers—and what a great way to recognize that boomers enjoy socializing with their pets as much as they do with other people!

- **Take into consideration that this generation is very concerned about "rights," including those of the consumer.** When designing your return policy or establishing your customer service department, be sure to include ways to communicate to boomers that you're taking everyone's rights and best interests into consideration in the problem resolution process. Author Angela Megasko wrote in *Creating the Ultimate Customer Experience*, "This generation wrote the book on protesting. The Vietnam War was an important event that shaped their values and ideals. Be ready to listen to this group because they are going to demand it."

GEN X

Gen X is the diversity generation. They grew up with no firsthand knowledge of the civil rights movement or segregation. They're also the first true computer generation. Many of them were "latchkey kids" (children of divorced, working parents), so they were alone after school much of the time. They learned to let themselves in at home, make themselves a snack, and do their own homework—all by themselves, with no help from an adult. All of these factors combined to make them very broad-minded, independent, and resourceful. As a result, they feel empowered by data and information as consumers.

To craft a strong and positive customer experience for these individuals, you must deliver the following six things:

- **A demonstrated commitment to diversity:** Showcase the diverse talent in your company and the populations you serve through your business. Use marketing materials, the causes you support, and the individuals you employ to demonstrate the various kinds of populations with whom you are involved. Make sure that your company has diverse talent at every level of the organization, not just the entry level. Because Gen Xers grew up with diversity, they want to see groups like women and minorities in management positions.

- **Technical excellence:** Make sure your electronic marketing, communication, order taking, and processing are up to date, functioning, and coordinated. Nothing frustrates this generation more than broken web links, outdated information, or a company's failure to have even the simplest of electronic tools, such as a website.
- **Informality:** Go ahead and use their first names when addressing members of this generation. Unlike many matures, this group will not be offended by this kind of informal interaction. Southwest Airlines has always done this, and it is in keeping with their casual, fun approach to business.
- **Self-reliance:** Gen X loves to be able to "do it themselves," by themselves, whether it's purchasing an item online, using the self-checkout lines at the grocery store, or watching a YouTube video that demonstrates how to hang wallpaper. Provide information about your product or service so that they can act more independently or be self-taught and achieve their own end product. Home Depot offers free classes for customers who want to tackle do-it-yourself projects but need advice. Teach Gen Xers how to do something themselves, and they will reward you with their loyalty.
- **Provision of data, standards, and transparency:** Information is power for Gen Xers, who assume that anything immeasurable is untrustworthy. If your product or service performs better than any other in its category, show them how that is so. A quip often used by former Secretary of Education Margaret Spellings speaks to many Gen Xers: "In God we trust. All others bring data."
- **Provision of real-time service (the "FedEx" test):** Many Gen Xers will apply the FedEx test to any transaction or purchase encounter; that is, they expect the service to be cheerful, fast, and efficient, with information and options in real time, online, 24/7. Even schools have had to adapt their customer experience to accommodate Gen X parents: the old "once-per-semester parent-teacher night" and snail-mail notifications no longer cut it. As Neil Howe wrote in "Meet Mr. and Mrs. Gen X: A New Parent Generation,"

"If Gen-X parents can get instant, real-time information on something as trivial as a package, why should they stay in the dark about their child's academic performance?" Geico Insurance nailed this with instant quotes for auto insurance online. Why wait for an agent to call you back with a quote when you can just get it now, yourself, instantly?

GEN Y

Gen Y is the most diverse and connected generation in history. They're not just tech-savvy; they are tech-*dependent*. Many members of this generation are actually *more* comfortable dealing with machines than with people. They are accustomed to having information and connectivity—to their friends, the news, and the world—at their fingertips, all the time.

I read an interesting article not long ago about the growth of Amtrak's ridership and revenue on the East Coast. Specifically, Amtrak could trace the rise in ridership to Gen Y. So many Gen Yers are riding the train on the East Coast for one singular reason: they don't have to turn off their electronic equipment, even for a few minutes, as you are required to do when you fly. For popular and fast East Coast routes like Washington, DC, to Philadelphia, Gen Y opts for taking the train—and the ability to have a Wi-Fi connection the entire way. What a great customer benefit to offer to those who value that above almost anything!

Here are the other aspects of customer experience that members of Gen Y value most:

- **Automation:** Why deal with people when you can just deal with a machine? Why deal with money when you can just swipe your credit card or debit card? Gen Y loves automation. Just as matures prefer to deal with someone face-to-face, Gen Y chooses technology and automation over human interaction. They simply see no need to involve anyone else when they can do something themselves.
- **Connectivity with their social circle:** Beyond just interacting via social networks, smart companies are figuring out ways to connect

their products or brands with Gen Y's friends. For example, Pepsi unveiled its Social Vending Machine, which taps into the popularity of social networking and gift gifting. This touch screen machine allows users to buy a free soda for a friend after entering his or her name, cell phone number, and a personalized text message. The machine sends the recipient the message and code to a free drink. Customers can also record a video message at the machine to include with the gift.

This connectivity is important to Gen Yers at all times—so important that even places that have been traditionally off-limits for connecting on your phone or online are no longer enforcing such parameters. "Tweet Seats" at the symphony and other performances are now being sold. Traditionally, live theater performances always started with an announcement to "turn off your phone." Now, theaters and the arts are actively promoting these special seats for those who want to share the theater experience with their friends *as it is happening*. The seats are in the back of the theater so that the light from the mobile phones doesn't disturb anyone seated behind them. Twitter users tweet throughout the performance, and theaters are reporting that the Tweet Seats are a huge success.

Even my dentist, Mark Whitfield of Aspen Dental House, has adapted to Gen Y's connectivity demands—and doing so has helped his business. My phone rang when I went in for a recent dental cleaning, and the hygienist immediately stopped what she was doing and asked, "Do you need to get that?" I didn't, but I was very impressed that she asked. When my dentist came in to complete the exam, I told him I was surprised that they were willing to halt the cleaning process to allow a patient to take a call. He told me that he'd learned that asking that simple question conveyed a powerful message to patients (we respect your time and how busy you are) and that rarely did anyone ever say, "Yes, I need to take this call." He told me that on the rare occasion that someone *did* need to take a call, the person was very quick about it—and it had never become a problem that put him behind schedule. Mark Whitfield gets it: if people feel that you understand their priorities, they'll feel a greater connection to you, which only increases their satisfaction and their loyalty. It also will increase your business.

Mark shared with me that he averages 30 new patients per month versus the 6 that the average dental practice of his size and tenure attains.

- **Customization for *everything*:** Gen Y demands that every item be customized to their tastes. To use another soft drink example, Coke's Freestyle machine allows users to customize a soft drink by mixing and matching different flavors. Customers can create up to 100 different flavor combinations with the machine. It's so popular that chatter on social networks such as Facebook and Twitter have users sharing their own concoctions, such as Gummy Bear and Creamsicle.
- **Selectivity:** Gen Y wants the ability to pick and choose what they want. After all, why buy a whole CD when you can purchase just the one song you like on iTunes? This "modular" approach to buying is very appealing to Gen Y. Car company Scion created it with automobiles, and other manufacturers followed. Gen Y would rather get just the accessories they want rather than pay for a package of preselected options that may or may not meet their needs.
- **Socializing at all times:** Members of Gen Y want to be with other people, even if they are strangers. The hotel industry is one that's had to radically modify their business to appeal to and attract Gen Y. The old business model of the traveling businessperson who has a drink in the lobby bar and then goes to the hotel room and watches TV or a movie is dead. Members of Gen Y do not want to sit in an enclosed bar, nor do they want to stay sequestered away in their hotel room. They are drawn to people and activity, even if it's activity in which they're not actively participating. For this reason, many hotels today have dramatically revamped their lobbies to make them more like open lounges and living rooms. There are an abundance of outlets to allow Gen Yers to bring their laptops to the lobby and hang out for hours. They can have a drink there as well, without having to go to a cheesy sports bar. They can people watch, surf the Internet, and chat with their friends on Facebook. They can strike up a conversation with others—or not. But even if they're traveling alone, they are not spending time alone in their rooms.

There's a triangle-shaped model that was once used to show that all consumers must compromise on what we want. It's called the Impossible Triangle because historically, you had to choose two of three attributes when buying a product or service: good, fast, or cheap. It was impossible to have all three. quality, schedule, or budget. But that's no longer necessarily true today—the Impossible Triangle no longer exists. And Gen Y has come to expect that they can—and should—be able to get all three sides of the triangle (Figure 9.1).

In the past, if you found a product or service that was good and fast, it wouldn't be cheap. If it was cheap and fast, it wouldn't be good. And if it was good and cheap, it wouldn't be fast. But the paradigm has changed, and we no longer have to assume that you have to pick which two attributes are most important to you.

Take iTunes, for example. The product's quality is superb (good); you can download a song in a matter of seconds (fast); and songs are cheap. Another B2C example would be developing photographic prints. It used to be that you dropped off film and a week later, could pick up your prints. Today, the process is not only good and cheap, it's also fast. The model can apply to both B2B and B2C products and processes. Gen Y sees no reason to settle for two of the three sides of the triangle. In fact, they *expect* to be able to have all three. When this is what a generation has come to expect and receive, then your business, product, or service needs to think about ways to deliver all three sides of the Impossible Triangle as well.

Each generation has its unique priorities, values, experiences and expectations. These shape their expectations of what they want from you in a customer experience. If you tailor the customer experience to deliver on the expectations for a specific generation, you'll grow your business with satisfied customers today—and their referrals tomorrow.

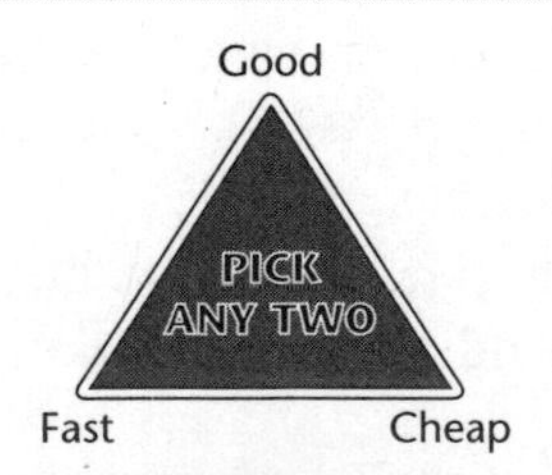

FIGURE 9.1 The "impossible triangle" no longer exists.

CHAPTER 10
Women and Families

One of my closest friends, Kenja Purkey, called me last summer and needed to talk. I mean, she *really* needed to talk. Kenja was, in fact, freaking out. You see, she had just learned that she was pregnant, and while this is typically happy news for a woman, Kenja is 40 years old ... with a 20-year-old daughter. In her own words: "Holy smokes. I was *this close* to being an empty nester and now, BAM! I'm going to be raising a child all over again." She was reeling from the news and what it meant for her, the plans that she and her husband had made (and would likely have to change), and how their lives overall would be very, *very* different.

It took a couple of weeks, but she adjusted to changes that this big news meant for her and her family. And then she kicked into planning gear and started doing her homework about what she'd need to buy to get ready for a new baby. After all, she had her last baby more than 20 years prior; it had been two decades since she had looked at or even really thought about baby items. And apparently, *everything* had changed over those decades. Kenja commented to me that when her daughter was born 20 years ago, "All I needed was all the basic stuff that anyone needs. You went out and bought it, and you were set. Now there is this 'culture of fear' that seems to permeate the baby business. All the products seem to stress their safety features and suggest that 'if you don't buy this particular item, your baby is at risk and you're not a good parent.'"

It's been interesting for me to watch her undergo this experience. I know what she means about the culture of fear that surrounds the baby and child industry. I've read a lot of articles about how moms today own the "safety" position, meaning that the number 1 priority for moms is to make sure their children are safe. They've moved from being called soccer moms to being called safety moms. They are so focused on safety that they have created vast networks as more and more moms connect online, form relationships, and share insights and tips with one another. They discuss what products to buy or not buy, and what they've heard about products or services from other moms. Many feel so strongly about sharing information that they have become "mommy bloggers," powerful online voices who blog extensively about child care, children's well-being, and their experiences as moms.

When I say these mommy bloggers have powerful voices, you better believe it. Some have hundreds of thousands of followers. In fact, an entirely new way of marketing to moms has developed because of this phenomenon: brands and companies are actively courting and cultivating influential mommy bloggers with the hopes that they will write favorably about their products. If a mommy gives a thumbs-up to a product on her blog that thousands of other moms read, sales go up. That's because women, especially mothers, tend to trust what other women have to say.

WOMEN TRUST OTHER WOMEN

It's not that women don't trust what *men* say; it's that women feel a deep connection to other females. And sometimes, we think that only another woman can understand what we're going through, what we're scared of, and what we need and want. Maybe it's because women tend to have so many different roles: wife, mother, daughter, friend, worker, head of household, homemaker, family nurturer, and more. Women do a lot for their families and have to meet a lot of demands. So do men, of course, but study after study has shown that, on average, women put more hours into running their households and taking care of their family each week than men do.

Therefore, women tend to feel that other women understand and empathize with those demands—and can guide them, honestly, in ways to manage those demands. Women also open up with other women and share personal stories or frustrations that they might not divulge to anyone else. They are counting on the fact that another woman will understand them, not judge them—and will, in fact, be able to help them.

Women don't think other women will lie to them. We count on one another to be candid and honest and steer us in the right direction. So you can see why the mommy bloggers can be so influential. If a woman respects another woman who says, "Go here and buy this" or "Don't ever buy this product or service," they tend to take that recommendation as gospel. We don't doubt it—we trust it. And we *appreciate* it.

What we get from such insider recommendations is *advice*. And that is where crafting the best customer experience for women starts: don't just give us information; give us *advice*.

PROVIDE ADVICE, NOT JUST INFORMATION

There is more information out there nowadays on any subject, at any time, than you could humanly process in 10 lifetimes. And this is true for all of us, not just women. The Internet has brought to your fingertips the entire universe of what's known. And although there is no denying how great and convenient that is, it's also tremendously overwhelming. Type "baby safety" into a search engine, and you'll get more than *half a million* responses. There is more information available than we can ever sift through or process. So we need a trusted guide, an interpreter, someone who can take all the information and distill down for us *just what we really need to know.*

The Pump Station & Nurtury is a breast-feeding resource center and baby boutique in Santa Monica, California, that's co-owned by lactation consultants Wendy Haldeman and Corky Harvey, both of whom are registered nurses specializing in maternal and newborn health. It is a successful business by any measure, but especially when you consider that they compete with vast entities such as Target, Babies "R" Us, and online retailers like Diapers.com. The Pump Station survives by offering a service that is not in danger of being taken over by the big retailers anytime soon: *assistance and education for nursing mothers*. They hold a monthly breast-feeding class that is consistently sold out. And they provide unbiased perspective on what new moms and dads *really* need to care for their baby.

A recent *New York Times* article that featured the Pump Station stated: "Over the last decade, as baby products have ballooned into a $9.8 billion industry, stores like the Pump Station have become more than just resource centers for nursing mothers. With an avalanche of baby care items on the market—how to decide between the Binky Most Like Mother Latex Pacifier and an Ortho-Pro Pacifier?—many parents are bewildered. And the Internet itself can be cluttered with conflicting information on sleep training and other baby care methods."

Mothers who turn to the Pump Station are often seeking a path through the chaos, along with products that a trusted source has approved. "When someone [says], 'Oh my God, there are 20,000 bottles out there,' we can tell them, 'But this bottle is going to be fabulous and will allow Dad to feed the baby and you to go back to work,'" says Cheryl Petran, the Pump Station's chief executive and a former buyer for Target and Montgomery Ward.

To help clear the confusion and provide their customers with the best possible experience when shopping their store, the Pump Station created a list of the owners' favorite products: "Corky and Wendy's Top 25 Recommended Baby Care Products."

"We do the research; we check it out," Wendy says. "Is this a good product? Is it safe? Is it ethical? Is it good for moms and babies? And then we'll bring it in."

And knowing that women trust women and moms trust moms, the store fosters a community environment of moms who interact with one another. As the *Times* article pointed out, "On any day, there may be a stroller jam of women in commiseration as they browse for organic swaddling blankets."

Not only does creating this kind of customer experience foster loyal, repeat, enthusiastic customers, it's also serious armor against bigger retailers and even a soft economy.

Referring to the list of recommended products they provide, Cheryl says, "Customers are willing to pay more for this 'stamp of approval.' Pricing isn't much of an issue"—even though they could find many of the store's items for less on sites such as Amazon.com or other retailers. That's because the Pump Station provides so much more than just products; they provide advice, guidance, resources, support, and a sense of community among nursing moms. You really can't put a price on that in most women's minds.

HARLEY-DAVIDSON CREATES A NEW EXPERIENCE—AND NEW RIDERS

Fifty-five-year-old Jo-Ellen Douglas had ridden a motorcycle with her husband for years. "I was just happy to be on the back," she said. "Now I've decided it's my turn." Harley-Davidson recognized that many women are intrigued by riding a motorcycle. Perhaps they are drawn to the sense of adventure and freedom or want an adrenaline rush. They may love the outdoors and the thrill of the open road. It doesn't matter what their reasons are; there is a sizable group of women interested in learning how to ride (and maybe even purchase) a motorcycle.

But the motorcycle world has traditionally been a man's one. And some women are intimidated by riding: they know that the bikes themselves can be heavy, and they are uncertain if they can handle one safely.

Harley-Davidson doesn't just want to sell motorcycles to women. They want women to become strong advocates of the brand and the rider experience. So they used the fears that women have about riding to create a customer experience that puts them at ease and makes them more comfortable with motorcycles in general.

The first thing they did was create the SuperLow, a bike designed to appeal to women and first-time riders. It's 150 pounds lighter than a typical Harley and has the lowest seat in Harley's 32-bike lineup, making it the easier to ride.

The second thing that Harley-Davidson did was work with its dealers to help women overcome some of their apprehension about safety. A few evenings a year, many of Harley's 650 U.S. dealers close their stores to men and hold women-only parties during which female staffers demystify the motorcycles. They hold free, no-sales-pressure classes; offer refreshments; and host a fashion show (because the Harley-Davidson brand is just as much about the apparel as it is about the bikes themselves). In March 2010, the company held about 500 such events, attracting 27,000 women, 11,000 of whom were in a Harley dealership for the first time. The company says it sold 3,000 bikes from the events that month.

One potential customer, Joanne DeGennaro, attended a dealer's Women's Garage Party for the first time. She said, "I have no idea what I'm doing. I mean the weight of it just intimidates me, you know?"

That night, however, she was able to sit on one of Harley's smaller bikes, a Sportster, and have a salesperson show her that it's easier to lift the 550-pound bike off its kickstand by turning the front wheel to the right. She said she now plans to sign up for Harley-Davidson's training class and get her license.

In 1995, just 2 percent of Harley-Davidson's owners were women. Today, 12 percent are. Furthermore, Harley enjoys a whopping 53 percentage point market share lead among female riders. Harley's products aren't cheap. If you want a less expensive motorcycle, you can buy a Yamaha or Kawasaki for a whole lot less. So for Harley to have a market share lead with women that eclipses their competitors by more than 50 percent is impressive indeed. And they've achieved this by creating an ongoing customer experience for women that addresses what women want and need: smaller, lighter bikes; a comfortable, no-pressure environment that allows them to learn and ask questions; and a fun event that connects them with other women who share their interest.

THE TRUTH CAN NEVER HURT YOU: PRACTICE FULL DISCLOSURE

A piece of practical advice when giving women an optimal customer experience: no matter what your product or service is, practice full disclosure. Don't ever try to misrepresent what your business or product or service can do. Women will find out if you "fudge" on your capabilities, and trust will be eroded at best or lost entirely at worst. It's not necessary to try to paint a better or enhanced picture of your product or service anyway. *Women can handle the truth*, even when you're telling them about a product shortcoming. What they can't handle—and strongly dislike—is the runaround or the feeling that a company has deceived them or given inaccurate information.

Here's an example: one of my clients is a female executive at a large electrical supply company and she travels extensively. She recently switched mobile phone providers, and in the process of shopping around for the right plan for her needs, she found that almost every carrier touted their extensive, "flawless" network of coverage. The reality is that no one carrier has *perfect* coast-to-coast coverage.

Some have more than others, but all have areas with weak, spotty, or virtually nonexistent coverage. Yet every salesperson she encountered boasted that his or her company's coverage was the best in the universe. My friend was skeptical, because she knew there was no way that this could be true. All she wanted was someone to give her the straight story so she could make a proper decision.

She found that honesty at AT&T. The salesperson took a unique approach: instead of telling her how strong their coverage is everywhere, he used a map of the United States to show her areas where AT&T's coverage is *less strong*. He positioned it as, "You've said you travel a great deal, and I just want you to know that in certain parts of Idaho, our network isn't as strong as it is in other places. I think it's important that you know this in case you travel to areas outside of Boise and other places in Idaho."

My friend was understandably impressed. No one else had even mentioned anything like that. Not only did the salesperson's candor make her trust him, but the information he provided allowed her to make an informed decision, which she weighed carefully. She rarely travels to Idaho, so having weaker coverage there wasn't likely to be an issue for her. And on the slim chance that she *would* travel to Idaho, she knew she wouldn't feel disappointed or deceived if she got off the plane and had only one bar of service. She'd be prepared for that, because the salesperson told her that might be the case. She ended up choosing AT&T as her provider, solely based on this information exchange. Other providers had lower rates and more comprehensive plans. But she liked the fact that she was fully educated about the service's capabilities and coverage. That allowed her to make an informed decision, one that would carry no surprises. And although being informed is a very empowering feeling for any customer, it's particularly empowering for women, as is having a range of choices and options.

SHOW ME ALL OPTIONS—YES, ALL 178 OF THEM, PLEASE

When I am doing a professional speaking engagement on the topic of customer service, one of the jokes I make is that there is a reason men's clothing comes in only three colors: black, navy, and khaki.

The crowd always laughs, because it *does* seem as if that's the case. Walk into a men's clothing store and look at suits; it's a sea of black, navy, and gray. The reason is that men like to have their choices narrowed for them. They can feel overwhelmed when there are too many options. Three seems to be almost the "magic number" for men: three main colors of clothing. Three main flavors of ice cream (chocolate, vanilla, or strawberry.) Three price points when it comes to electronics (good, better, and best). For whatever reason, this formulaic approach seems to work well with men.

Precisely the opposite is true when it comes to women: we like to see *all the options* available to us. And we don't care if that's 3 or 33 or 300. Women want to make an informed choice, and seeing every single possibility allows us to do just that. Furthermore, we don't easily become overwhelmed by lots of choices. In fact, it almost seems to have the opposite effect on us: we're able to more easily narrow down or weed out what we *don't* want by seeing all options. We like looking at a wide array of clothing options and colors. We love having 20 or more ice cream flavors to choose from. The more choices we have, the better! Extensive choice doesn't overwhelm us; it appeals to us.

So don't shy away from spending time reviewing *all options* with your female customers and prospects. They'll greatly appreciate the information; it won't overwhelm or confuse them. In fact, your willingness to share all the information will likely create a sale, as well as a *customer relationship* with a woman who trusts you and feels she made the right decision for what she needs, based on all available options.

FAMILIES

Many women are moms, and as such, many believe that taking care of their family's well-being is a key part of their role. So don't overlook women's families when you are crafting an optimal customer experience for them. If you can cater to and ensure that a family is enjoying your product or service, I can pretty much guarantee that you'll win over the mom. And that's important, because statistics show that women make 80 percent of household buying decisions.

Some companies have realized the "power of the family" when it comes to making women feel great about their brands. They might do so by providing parking spots closest to the store for expectant moms or families or by offering child care for parents while they shop. Whatever the situation or service, catering to the family can pay dividends in cultivating satisfaction and loyalty.

Popular furniture store IKEA, known for affordable and contemporary offerings, has free child care for up to 90 minutes at their Småland Play Area. Children who meet the height requirement (roughly 36 inches to 50 inches, depending on the store) can play in a pit full of plastic balls, watch videos, read books, play with puppets (that IKEA sells, of course), or work on craft projects under the supervision of IKEA employees. While kids play in Småland, often referred to as the ball room, their parents browse the store or hang out in the café using the free Wi-Fi. The idea behind Småland, of course, is to distract the children long enough to let the parents shop.

"Lately, we've seen an increase in a lot of new parents," said Yumiko Whitaker, public relations manager for IKEA's Orange County stores in California. "They're getting out of the house, and we're providing an environment that gives them a break."

But what if customers take advantage of a perk like this? What if they don't buy a thing and just use IKEA as a free babysitting service? "We certainly hope they'll purchase some IKEA products," said Mona Astra Liss, the director of public relations for IKEA in the United States. "But if they don't, we still feel satisfied we introduced them to IKEA."

This low-pressure retail strategy, combined with IKEA's reputation for selling low-priced furniture, seems to be working. "At a time when families are cutting back on vacations and restaurant visits, an outing to IKEA suddenly sounds quite attractive—especially when you throw in free babysitting and cheap food," said Natalie Berg, a senior retail analyst at Planet Retail, a London-based consulting group.

Parents are not allowed to leave the store after dropping off their children at Småland, and they must provide their mobile phone numbers. The IKEA in Round Rock, Texas, gives parents a beeper and pages them when their child's time in the play area is up. If they don't respond to the page, an announcement is made over the public address system. "If it takes too long, we call them on their cell phone," said Danielle Komisar, who oversees Småland at the Round Rock store. "Sometimes they're simply stuck in the checkout line."

Catering to family needs makes a big impression on every member, but it especially impresses the woman who is nurturing that family. She's going to remember the way you treated her family, and she'll reward you with her business.

Caring for any family is a challenge, but it can be especially tough for moms who have a family member with a disability. In these cases, you have a huge opportunity to create a customer experience that is sensitive and caring—as well as lucrative.

THOSE WITH DISABILITIES

It's said that one in four people suffer from mental illness. And millions of people have physical disabilities. Some disabilities are obvious, and some are not. A customer's disability may prevent him or her from doing business with you. But sometimes you can make small, low-cost, or even no-cost tweaks to your product or service to make it user-friendly for those with disabilities. Let me give you an example.

The Segway, a two-wheeled self-balancing battery-powered electric vehicle, is a wonderful way for amputees to get around and be mobile. It's fast and nimble. And although anyone can use a Segway, it's a product that makes sense for those without legs. Consequently, it's a popular item for veterans who have lost a leg (or both) through their military service. I was moved by an article I read recently about a man who is a double amputee and had a custom seat made for his Segway that fits his unique needs. But in order to transport the Segway, he requires assistance from others. He needed help loading and unloading the Segway into a vehicle. Most of us like to be able to do things ourselves, without having to depend on others. So although having a Segway afforded this man a great deal of mobility, he still needed others to assist him in using it. Enter the SegVator: a specially created vehicle designed to transport Segways that even recharges the Segway when it is being driven.

Two things in this article impressed me greatly: First, the SegVator was designed for ease of use, *regardless of varying physical abilities.* It easily loads and unloads a Segway so that a *person does not need assistance from another in order to transport the Segway.* Second, it's sold through the Segway authorized dealer network. Even though SegVator is not manufactured by Segway, the company's dealers understood immediately that they could provide a better customer solution and enhanced experience by affiliating with SegVator. It's doesn't change the brand's focus on their core product for Segway dealers to offer the SegVator at their dealerships, but it certainly enhances that product when a dealer can demonstrate a *comprehensive solution* to a customer. Imagine that you don't have legs. And here's a product that can assist you—the Segway. And here is *another* product that can assist you *even more* because now you can take your Segway anywhere you can drive. *And you can do it by yourself.*

Is there a commercial aspect to this? Of course there is. The makers of SegVator want to sell their product. But the Segway dealer network recognized that they can serve their disabled customers *better* by offering a product that they do not even manufacture because it *solves a problem* their customers may have. They are still focused on their core business, selling Segways, but they demonstrate that they understand a disabled individual's needs and provide a solution by tweaking their product offering with the SegVator.

There is a "sales" aspect to the customer experience in this example. Segway is expanding their business by reaching customers they might not otherwise have reached. They are able to sell them something that *complements* their core product and helps meet the needs of amputees and others with disabilities. There's nothing wrong with that, as long as what your customer experiences is respectful and appropriate. It's perfectly okay to develop or sell a product or service for a new customer group, provided you don't exploit or behave in an insensitive manner toward that customer. *Meeting needs is an essential component of having a great customer experience.* After all, it doesn't matter how nice you are to me if you simply can't meet my needs. But when you couple kindness, dignity, and sensitivity with filling a need, you've got a pretty unbeatable combination.

Take AMC Theatres as another example. This nationwide chain of movie theaters in the United States partnered with the Autism Society to develop a new movie experience for those with autism. Autistic children often can't go to a regular movie because the sensory experience (a loud movie, coupled with a dark theater) can overwhelm or frighten them. Theater etiquette demands silence and stillness so that all may enjoy the movie, and many autistic children simply can't control their verbal impulses or sit still for an extended period of time.

So AMC Theatres created monthly "sensory-friendly films" to allow families affected by autism and other disabilities to enjoy their favorite movies in a safe and accepting environment. These auditoriums have their lights brought up and the sound turned down; families are able to bring in their own gluten-free, casein-free snacks (many believe there is a link between autism and these dietary components); and the theater doesn't show any previews or advertisements before the movie. In addition, audience members are welcome to get up and dance, walk, shout, or sing; in other words, AMC does not enforce their silence policy unless the safety of the audience is questioned.

Imagine what a wonderful experience it is for families with autistic and special needs children to go to a movie and enjoy it, knowing that their child is in an environment that understands, accepts, and welcomes them as customers. And this large theater chain not only is sensitive to customers with disabilities but has actually tweaked its product offering to give special needs customers the movie experience. They *created* a special movie time just for those with autism and other related disabilities. This offering doesn't change AMC Theatre's core focus on mainstream movies. It simply adds a product to their mix that quietly but profoundly demonstrates that they see, respect, value, and welcome all customers.

And crafting this customer experience probably cost AMC Theatre very little. The steps that they take to make the experience appropriate for the audience really don't cost them anything: adjusting the sound and lighting, allowing children to make noise and move about. And although they may lose a small amount of revenue by allowing parents to bring in snacks for their kids and by eliminating the previews and ads, it's surely offset by those parents' appreciation and loyalty. When a company has shown that kind of sensitivity to your child's needs, why would you take your business anywhere else? I would imagine that going to AMC Theatres is a regular part of family entertainment for families with autistic kids—and that they get lots of customers who come for every special showing.

You don't always have to create a *new* product or service to provide an effective customer experience. Sometimes you just need to think through your infrastructure to determine whether you are easy to do business with. Take Shoplet.com, for example, a comprehensive e-retailer that sells more than 400,000 products online. From office supplies and furniture, to tools and hardware, to cleaning and office break room supplies, Shoplet.com sells it. They have a live chat function on their site that anyone can use. Shoplet.com has found that this function is very useful for their hearing-impaired customers, as well as customers who cannot use the phone at work. The chat function provides an instant interaction between customers with a question and a live customer service representative.

The most unique function that customers use their chat for is language translation. Although the chat feature itself cannot translate on its own, customer service reps can cut and paste foreign language dialogue from the chat box into Google Translate and vice versa. This allows customers who are not fluent (or comfortable) in English to communicate effectively with customer service associates. Shoplet.com chief executive officer (CEO) Tony Ellison says, "Not all of our customers' first language is English. Many customers use our online chat feature to reach out to our customer service in their native language. Shoplet.com receives many thanks from these customers for accommodating them in the language they are most comfortable with." What a great way to personalize and enhance the customer service experience!

Their representatives are also seasoned communicators on TTY, the device that allows users to type their communication rather than speak it. TTY is widely used by the elderly, those with hearing impairments, and those who have difficulty speaking or who cannot speak.

As an e-retailer, Shoplet.com needs to be able to communicate with customers—*all* customers—online. Brick-and-mortar stores staffed with associates don't exist. Between their live chat function and their TTY communications, they can serve all of their customers effectively. By seeing their infrastructure from the point of view of those whose primary language is not English and those who have hearing or speaking impairments, Shoplet.com developed systems and tools that allow them to craft the best possible customer experience.

Sometimes, crafting an exceptional customer experience is simply about going above and beyond to help someone do business with you. One of my friends, William Siskron, is the manager of a bank in Dallas. He told me about a customer of theirs who is partially deaf; she is *very* hard of hearing. She came into the bank to express concern that someone was using her banking information fraudulently. Because she is hard of hearing, my friend wrote everything down for her so that he was able to clearly communicate with her on this serious matter. The situation became more complicated, however, as they tried to file the appropriate fraud claims to certain departments. Associates in those departments wanted to speak directly to the customer, who could not hear a word they were saying. So William kept writing his questions and those of other departments for her. They went back and forth like this for nearly two weeks.

At some point, William learned that she had an electronic translator machine that would allow her to call into the bank to speak to them, which meant she wouldn't have to come into the bank every day as she had been. He also learned that she did not know how to set up the machine, and not having anyone to help her, she simply hadn't done it. William told her to bring the machine in with her the next day, and they would help set it up. He sat down with this customer for an extended period of time, even calling the machine's customer service department, and finally got it working properly. As he later told me, "This was a unique experience, but we are so glad we were able to help her. Simply taking the time to help this client set up a service in order to be able to communicate with us and not have to come to the bank every day meant the world to this customer. I think it is something we will likely run into more and more as our clientele gets older."

Clearly, none of this was part of the bank's responsibility. Nowhere in any of the bank employees' job descriptions does it say that they are required to help a customer set up electronic equipment for the hard of hearing. But in this case, it was the right thing to do. It also cost them nothing but a little bit of time to do it—and it gained them a happy, satisfied, loyal customer who will find it easier than ever to do business with them. They went over and above to take care of their customer, who will reward them with continued business and loyalty.

Crafting a superior customer experience for anyone is important. It can be even more important for your customers with physical or mental challenges. In fact, it may determine their ability to do business with you in the first place. And it may cement loyalty and future business in a way that nothing else can.

CHAPTER 11
Hispanics/Latinos

The largest ethnic minority in the United States is Hispanics. The population now numbers more than 50 million, something that definitely catches the attention of virtually every brand, product, company, and organization. Everyone in business wants to know how to tap into the Hispanic (or Latino, if you prefer) market, and it's no wonder; it just makes good business sense to pay attention to a consumer segment of this magnitude.

Hispanics are an enormously desirable consumer target because of what I refer to as the 3 Ls: it is a large, lucrative, and loyal segment. They have a substantial population; to put 50 million in context for you, it makes *the United States the second largest Hispanic country in the world*—second only to Mexico. The Hispanic market is also a very lucrative one; with solidly middle-class household income and significant purchasing power, it's no wonder companies and brands are salivating over this consumer. And, of course, everyone wants a loyal customer. You always want to retain a customer after spending precious resources marketing to, attracting, and selling to him or her. You want this customer to keep coming back for more. Numerous studies have shown that when Hispanics have a good customer experience, they don't just become loyal customers; they make *fiercely* loyal customers.

The Hispanic market is large, lucrative, and loyal—and those are the three Ls that every business wants their customers to be.

So what defines a good customer experience for Hispanics? Many things, of course, such as a welcoming invitation to do business through targeted marketing. I devote an extensive chapter in my book *How to Market to People Not Like You: "Know It or Blow It" Rules for Reaching Diverse Customers* to a discussion of how to effectively market to the Hispanic consumer. I offer key steps as well as an acculturation model that breaks the Hispanic market segment into four primary subsegments. But in this chapter, I want to focus on the *customer experience—aside* from marketing. I am going to assume that you have either already been marketing effectively to Hispanics or perhaps haven't been doing any dedicated Hispanic marketing but that you nonetheless have a significant Hispanic customer base or clientele whose experience you want to enhance.

"PRESS 1 FOR ENGLISH" ISN'T A FAD

One of the first areas you need to address to provide a superior experience for your Hispanic customers is language. The latest study from global market research company Synovate shows that 60 percent of all Hispanic adults in the United States are foreign-born. So if you're foreign-born, chances are that your native language is Spanish. And even if you become fluent in English, your mother tongue will *always* be Spanish, so it's a pretty safe bet that Spanish is most foreign-born Hispanics' preferred language.

This is particularly important if what you sell is the slightest bit complicated, is important, requires a contract, or has a layered buying process. For example, buying a new or used automobile is much more complicated—and important—than buying a burger. Not only does the vehicle cost thousands of dollars more than a hamburger, but the transaction itself is complex. You need to negotiate a price, determine how you'll pay for the car (i.e., pay cash or finance it), figure out whether you qualify for a loan or credit, discuss additional options such as extended warranties and accessories, and so on. On top of that, most people don't buy a vehicle very often. Once you make that purchase decision, you're out of the market until the next time you need a car or truck, which is probably going to be years, maybe even a decade.

A burger, on the other hand, is in what we call a low consideration category. Most people don't agonize over where to buy one. They're hungry, so they get one. And if the burger is only average in its taste, well, so what? It's just a burger. You may be out a few bucks if you don't like the burger, but it's not a big deal. You can always try a different one at a different place the next day.

So imagine that you are a foreign-born Hispanic customer who's lived in the United States for 10 years. In that time, you've learned quite a bit of English and are functionally fluent, meaning you can function in an English-speaking society. But that doesn't mean that you *comprehend* everything in English the same way a native speaker does. You may understand 80 or 90 percent of a purchase conversation or sales process, but what about the other 10 to 20 percent? Shouldn't your goal as a business owner be to ensure that your customers who speak or prefer Spanish *fully know and understand* the product or service they're buying? A crucial component of customer satisfaction is to have *confidence in what you're buying in the first place*. It's comforting—and empowering—to feel as though you have made an intelligent, informed decision. This isn't a unique characteristic of Hispanic consumers. In the last chapter, I talked about how important information is to women when making purchase decisions as well. Most people feel most comfortable when they feel informed. How can you make a fully informed decision if you don't even understand 100 percent of the conversation about a product's features, attributes, and benefits?

Having someone on your staff who speaks Spanish gives you the ability to communicate *fully*, not just partially, with individuals who are native Spanish speakers. Think of how important this aspect is when it comes to understanding things like contracts, warranties, and policies. You want your customers to know what they are buying, how it works, why it's the best product or service for their needs, what their rights are, what *your* rights are, and more. The better informed and educated your customers are, the more likely they are not only to buy from you but to have a totally satisfactory experience with you. If your customer can talk with someone in his or her language, that person can ask all of his or her questions—and understand all the responses. This gives the customer a significantly greater opportunity to forge a bond with the salesperson or customer service representative providing help. The customer will be more comfortable with the entire process. And that will most certainly impact your ability to make—and *keep*—a sale.

In addition, many Hispanic families shop and make purchases together. It's not uncommon for the entire family to weigh in on whether to buy a product and which one. And there are often differing levels of English proficiency in the same family. For example, you may have a multigenerational Hispanic family with a foreign-born grandma, mom, and dad but American–born children. In that case, the kids are probably completely bilingual because they are being educated in English at school, but the family most likely speaks Spanish at home, all or much of the time.

I live in Texas, where the Hispanic population is approaching nearly half of the state's total population. I see a family dynamic all the time wherein bilingual children often serve as the "family translators." But do you really want an eight-year-old kid trying to explain your product's or service's benefits—or the ins and outs of your warranty or return policy—to the rest of the family? Wouldn't it make more sense to be able to provide the customer experience in Spanish for those who prefer it?

So, if you have Hispanic customers, you'll want to hire someone who can speak Spanish. It's best if that individual is bilingual so that he or she can also assist customers in English. Due to the growth of the Hispanic population, bilingual associates are in great demand these days. You know how hard it is to find reliable employees with a strong work ethic, who have good heads on their shoulders, and who are resourceful and customer-focused. Now you're adding a language criterion to that list as well—and you may feel like you are looking for a needle in a haystack. But don't hire the *wrong person* just because that person speaks Spanish. Make sure you are hiring someone who has all the skills and personality qualities you look for in an associate, and *then* consider that person's language skills in the hiring decision. I have seen far too many clients hire someone with language skills (such as the ability to speak Chinese, Vietnamese, or Spanish) only to dismiss the person later because he or she wasn't well suited to the job, the company, or the customers. In all cases, the company was so desperate for someone who could speak another language that the person hiring overlooked flaws, personality clashes, and/or gaps in skills.

But the search for a good bilingual associate will pay off if you have Hispanic customers. Not only will that individual be able to speak the language your customers either want or need, but he or she will most likely have a solid grasp of cultural nuances that can factor into the customer experience equation.

And that leads to the next thing you want to consider when providing an exceptional customer experience for your Hispanic customers: understanding cultural differences. Although it's never a good idea to generalize any group's behavior or values, many studies and surveys have shown that Hispanics, *regardless of language preference*, do share some common traits and attributes when making shopping and purchase decisions. Studies have found that the majority of Hispanics either "agree" or "strongly agree" with key statements about their attitudes toward shopping and buying, such as:

- I'm more likely to shop/do business in a place that **"makes me feel welcome."**
- I'm more likely to shop/do business in a place that is **"pleasant to be in."**
- I'm **more likely to have more questions** about a product or service than non-Hispanics.
- "I appreciate **being given all the time I need** to make a decision."
- **"Personal service** is more important than speed and efficiency."

How might some of these values manifest themselves in your store, restaurant, or business? It's about making sure your business isn't just Latino-ready but that it's also Latino-friendly. And there's a significant difference between the two.

LATINO-READY

Being Latino-ready means that your business infrastructure can support doing business in Spanish. As already discussed, that means having someone on staff who can speak Spanish. This is the cornerstone of truly being able to attract Hispanic consumers to your business and serve them effectively. If you market to Hispanics, they'll come. And when they do, many will need or want to speak Spanish. If you don't have anyone who can assist Hispanic customers in their native language, you've essentially just driven them into a brick wall. Employing Spanish-speaking personnel—whether in a retail store or at a customer service call center—shows that you are prepared to serve the Spanish-speaking customer in his or her language of preference. When you have the opportunity to hire someone, advertise for and interview bilingual people. Schools and community colleges are great places to recruit, because many have a growing Hispanic student body. Spanish media in most places also offer free job postings for employers, and the media outlet (radio station, newspaper, and so on) will usually also translate your ad posting at no charge. Catholic churches that hold services in Spanish and the Hispanic Chamber of Commerce are also great places to post ads. Be sure your ads spell out that you need bilingual skills, not just Spanish-speaking; otherwise, you'll end up with candidates who speak Spanish but *not* English.

What if you're a small-business owner and you have someone on your staff who speaks Spanish but you have two locations? Your bilingual employee can't be in two places at one time. In that case, you can develop a process that lets customers know that you're going to help them in Spanish, but through a bit of an unconventional "technique." National mattress retailer Mattress Firm developed a process that assisted both their customers and their employees. When a Spanish-speaking customer walked into a store where no one on staff spoke Spanish, an associate would smile, greet the person, and hand him or her a card that was printed in Spanish that read: *"Hi! I don't speak Spanish, but I'm going to call someone at another of our locations who does. In the meantime, please fill out the back of this card so that we may serve you better."* The back of the card had a bilingual checklist that asked what the customer was looking for (twin, full, queen-, or king-size mattress), whether the customer has any special needs or problems (back pain, neck pain, and so on), whether the customer prefers a soft or firm mattress, and so forth. The customers loved that the card was professionally printed and well thought out and that they were being helped in Spanish. And the sales associates loved it too. The English-speaking employee could call a bilingual associate and let him or her know what the customer's needs were (e.g., "The customer wants a queen-size mattress, extra firm"). Together, the team would help the customer and close the sale. Their process wasn't very sophisticated, but it was effective and it helped increase sales. It also improved employee morale because English-speaking associates now had a way to work with Hispanic customers that they'd never had before.

Latino-ready also can include things like having information, literature, or a website in Spanish; having signage and policies in Spanish; and perhaps even having specific products that cater to Hispanic needs or tastes. Let me give you an example.

Laredo, Texas, is right on the border of Texas and Mexico. As such, 98 percent of the population of Laredo is Hispanic and the local Walmart stores reflect this market's needs and consumer tastes. Not only is virtually everyone who works at the stores bilingual, but the signage in the stores is all bilingual and all policies—such as warranties, returns, and exchanges—are posted in both Spanish and English. This makes it easy for their clientele to do business with Walmart. Their stores are Latino-ready.

Even their product offerings and selections cater to Hispanic needs and tastes. For example, a few years ago, the general manager of one of Laredo's Walmarts gave a fascinating interview on how he'd observed that Hispanic shoppers differ from non-Hispanic shoppers. He noted that brightly colored blouses sell better than neutrals and that women's jeans were not selling well at all. Why? Because the women's jeans that Walmart stocked at the time didn't flatter many Hispanic women's figures. You see, many Hispanic women have smaller waists and larger hips than non-Hispanic women. So although these jeans might sell well at the Des Moines or Boise Walmarts, they gapped at the waist and were too tight through the hips on the majority of Laredo's Hispanic women shoppers. But Walmart's purchasing power comes from buying large quantities of products at low prices and distributing those products throughout all of their stores, which is why Walmart was stocking these particular jeans. This savvy store manager was somehow able to rectify this with his corporate buyers, and they changed their inventory mix to better suit the needs of Hispanic women's bodies. They started stocking jeans that were cut smaller in the waist and were more forgiving in the hips. And guess what? The jeans started flying off the shelves.

Even the Girl Scouts have expanded their cookie offerings with Hispanic-inspired flavors and varieties. One of their most popular cookies nowadays is *dulce de leche*, which has a caramel flavor and is made with goat's milk instead of cow's milk. These Girl Scout cookies have been created specifically for Hispanic palates, as they are less sweet and sugary than most cookies you'd buy or find in a store in the United States. American cookies are simply too sweet for many Hispanics, who prefer cookies made with less sugar and more subtle flavors, like vanilla and cinnamon. And, of course, the box features photos of Hispanic-looking girls.

Being Latino-ready is a crucial part of providing an exceptional customer service experience for your Hispanic customers. But it's not the *only* step you need to take. You also need to make sure your business is Latino-friendly.

LATINO-FRIENDLY

Just as important as being Latino-ready is being Latino-*friendly* to effectively cultivate Hispanic customers. In fact, some would say that being Latino-friendly is *more* important. That's because friendliness is universal and is always appreciated. You can travel the world over and not speak any language other than your own, and you will find yourself gravitating toward the friendly people, businesses, restaurants, and places that make you feel welcome.

Being Latino-friendly doesn't cost a thing. It just requires that you make your business a place where Hispanic customers feel welcome and appreciated. And just like the Latino-ready step, it starts with your staff. Even if no one on your staff speaks Spanish, they can be Latino-friendly simply by making eye contact and showing warmth, sincerity, helpfulness, and personal service. Essentially, it's all the basics of good customer service and good common sense rolled into one.

A store manager at Sherwin-Williams, the largest retail paint company in the world, told me that he didn't have anyone on staff who spoke Spanish at his store in Dallas. However, he had a large and thriving clientele of Hispanic customers. I asked him how he served and handled his customers. "We make sure they know that we want their business," he told me. "We make them feel valued and welcome. When they walk in the door, we make eye contact, smile, and say '*¡Hola!*' (*Hola* is Spanish for 'hi'). When they see us smiling and greeting them, they smile back and we start to help them. Sometimes there is a bit of a communication gap, but between our efforts and the customer's, we can always work it out. We know a few words in Spanish—they know a few words in English. They tend to shop as a family, so we have lollipops for the kids and coloring books for them, too. You see, mixing paint can take a while, so we want to make sure the kids don't get bored. And the parents really appreciate that. When they leave, we always say '*¡Gracias!*' and they always laugh and smile. They like coming to our store, and we know this because they bring others—the referral business is huge."

Comments like this are typical. Businesses like this Sherwin-Williams store are successful with Hispanic customers not because they are Latino-ready but because they are Latino-friendly. There are reasons why your business may not be very Latino-ready: perhaps it's difficult to find bilingual staff, or you have no control over the products and services you provide. But there is *no reason* to not be Latino-friendly. It will cover a multitude of shortcomings, and it positions you better in the customers' eyes than any amount of marketing you can do. It is possible to be Latino-friendly without being Latino-ready and vice versa. Believe me, if you can be only one of those, be Latino-friendly. Here's why.

There is a large national bank that you likely know or have heard of; they are everywhere in the United States. Several years ago, they got very serious about their Hispanic marketing efforts, and this bank is now very, very Latino-ready. Everything you could want is available in Spanish: their website, the ability to do online banking in Spanish, and all their brochures. Their point-of-sale materials in the bank are all bilingual, their call centers are staffed with bilingual operators and customer care professionals, and they offer highly competitive rates for wiring money. You get the picture; they are about as Latino-ready as a business can be.

One day, I was in one of this bank's branches, waiting in line behind a Hispanic man. He had a check to cash and his U.S. passport for identification; however, he didn't have a driver's license. Perhaps he didn't have a car. After all, what do you need a driver's license for if you don't own a car or drive? And it seems obvious to me that a *federally issued passport* trumps a state-issued driver's license as a valid form of ID anyway. The man put his check and his passport down in front of the teller and said, "Please." It was pretty clear what he wanted: to either deposit or cash the check. The teller folded her arms across her chest, looked at him, and in a loud and snotty voice said, *"DRIVER'S LICENSE!"* He shook his head and held out his passport again, as if to say, "I don't have a license, but I have *this.*" But she was unmovable. She stood there, arms crossed, every bit of her body language implying that she knew exactly what he wanted but she sure wasn't going to try to help or even meet him halfway. The customer stood there and again said, "Please," and the teller raised her voice and yelled, loudly enough for everyone to hear, "No driver's license? No cash-o check-o!" The customer may not have spoken English well, but he knew he was being insulted and mocked and, after what felt like an hour to me but was probably just a few seconds, he left.

That may be the end of his story, but my part continues. When I walked up to the same teller, she sweetly asked me how she could help me. Here's how our conversation went:

Me: "Just a second. I have a question. Why didn't you cash that man's check?"
Teller: "Well, he didn't have a driver's license."
Me: (pivoting, looking all around the bank) "Hmm ... I don't see any signs stating that if you want to cash a check, you have to have a driver's license. That's your policy? I don't see that posted anywhere. In fact, I cash checks here all the time, and no one ever asks me for my driver's license."
Teller: "Well, those people shouldn't be here anyway."

Those people? *Those* people? People with U.S. passports? No, of course not. She meant Hispanics. It was outrageous. It was offensive. And it was wrong. But the point is this: that bank was Latino-*ready* in almost every way. However, they were *not* Latino-friendly. It all came down to that one teller's actions and behavior. She is the person with whom this customer had the experience; therefore, she *is* the bank to him. And all the effort that they put into being operationally ready—all the money they sunk into brochures, collateral materials, website, and so on—is *wasted* if that's what the customer's experience is like.

In fact, the bank's Latino-readiness made the situation even worse. Because when you've made your business Latino-ready and are actively promoting your business to Hispanics, especially in Spanish, you're sending a message that says: "We *want* your business. Come to us. We're ready to help and we can serve you—in Spanish." To set the consumer's expectations in one way and then to deliver an experience that makes that same consumer feel unwelcome and unwanted is confusing, as well as misleading. Consumers will feel as if they've been lied to—and they have! It's a complete waste of your time and money if you are Latino-ready but not Latino-friendly.

Let me tell you another story, with a different outcome. It's about an auction house in Indiana called Christy's, one of the largest and most successful independent auction houses in the country. It's owned by a man named Jack Christy, who may be one of the nicest, kindest, and smartest people I've ever met. Christy's was selected for a special pilot program by the National Auctioneers Association (NAA). The NAA wanted to do an exploratory program to see if they could increase the number of Hispanics attending auctions, and they hired us to help them. Auction houses auction off all kinds of items, from property to automobiles to collector's items, household items—you name it. The NAA selected a few of their best auction owners to participate in this program, and that's how I met Jack.

Jack's auction house is located in Indianapolis. At the time of the pilot program, he did not have anyone on his staff who spoke Spanish. They weren't Latino-ready at all. But Jack saw the business opportunity that Hispanic residents in the area represented, and he knew he could grow his business if he could get them to experience an auction at his facility. The first thing he did, though, was have a kickoff meeting to let all of his employees know about the pilot program. He filled them in on what they were trying to accomplish and the important role each and every one of them played in making these new customers "feel like they've come to the right place." Jack informed them of Hispanic population and growth numbers to make it crystal clear what made this program so important. He shared with them every element of what they'd be doing, so they were informed and had a chance to ask questions. And he signed everyone up for lunchtime Spanish lessons with a local teacher who came to their facility weekly to teach basic Spanish phrases.

The employees *loved* it. They all understood what was going on and why and what was expected of them, and they were excited to be part of a national "test" program. About a month after the kickoff meeting, my staff went to Indianapolis for a follow-up meeting with Jack and his team. I got a call from one of our associates there who excitedly told me, "Kelly, you won't believe it! As Jack was walking us to the conference room today, we noticed little brightly colored

Post-it Notes stuck on *everything*—on the walls, on pictures, on windows, on the refrigerator in their break room, even on the copier!"

I replied, "Post-it Notes? What for? What do they say?"

And my employee replied, "They have the Spanish word for that item on them! So the Post-it Note on the window says *'ventana'* and the note on the light switch says *'luz.'* It's so amazing and Jack said it was the employees' idea! They're all so into it and are trying so hard to be Latino-friendly."

Jack later told me that as their Hispanic clientele grew, their Spanish-speaking customers would smile about the notes and often helped with the proper word for an object. Several customers even asked for the English word to be added to the notes so that they, too, could pick up the words. Now *that* is Latino-friendly! Why would a Hispanic customer want to do business anywhere else?

That example shows how even the little things can make your business Latino-friendly. So don't be afraid to try. Put your heart into it and give it your best and warmest effort. You'll be rewarded. And to get you started, here's a checklist of some things to consider as you think about preparing your business to serve Hispanic customers:

Latino-Ready

- Hire bilingual, Spanish-speaking staff (at least one individual to start, then others to make sure you have adequate coverage).
- Have bilingual associates record their voicemail greetings in Spanish and English.
- Have telephone system options in Spanish.
- Provide information on your website in Spanish, even if it's just one page of FAQs.
- Offer products that may be right for Hispanic needs and tastes.

Latino-Friendly

- Offer cultural sensitivity training for employees. For example, *"Talking louder does not make someone bilingual"* (an actual customer comment from a Hispanic focus group).
- Provide customer service and customer care training: smiling, greeting customers in a welcoming, friendly manner.

- Accommodate families shopping and/or making decisions together (provide more chairs in a waiting room or office or provide small toys for kids).
- Be patient with questions. Often Hispanic customers will have more questions about a product or service than non-Hispanic customers.
- Adjust your hours, if necessary. An evening appointment may need to be 8 PM rather than 6 PM to accommodate a Hispanic customer's schedule, since many Hispanics work in the hospitality or construction or service businesses, where hours are long, and not necessarily 9 AM to 5 PM. Therefore, if you're an insurance agent or a realtor and want to meet with someone "after work" to sell him or her insurance or show a home, be aware that it may not be possible for him or her to meet you at 6 PM. A Hispanic customer may need to meet you considerably later than that. (We hear time and time again in focus groups that an "optimal evening appointment is 8 PM.")

LA FAMILIA (THE FAMILY) IS KEY

Everyone likes to think that they put their family first. Hispanic customers put special emphasis on your treatment of the whole family, which can make or break your sale and determine how the customer views the entire experience. Even when family members aren't the ones who will use the product or service directly, their opinion matters and can sway the decision-making process. We learned from Mattress Firm managers and sales associates that the kids in the family often help decide which mattress to buy, even though the mattress was for mom and dad and they wouldn't even necessarily ever be sleeping on it. They weren't just along on the shopping trip; they were active participants in the purchasing process.

Once you know and understand this important family dynamic, you can cater to it. For instance, several years ago, one of my employees and her husband were looking for a new SUV. They were torn between two different brands, a Chevy model and a Toyota model. There were things they liked about both, and they were having a hard time deciding which to buy. This employee and her family, including her husband, are Hispanic. During the shopping process, they spent considerable time at the competing dealerships, learning about the vehicles, test-driving them, and talking with the sales associates. They didn't want to make a rash decision, since both SUVs were priced at more than $40,000, a substantial purchase. So they visited each dealership a couple of times over the course of a few days. This allowed them to digest the information they got and really think it over.

My employee brought along her mother, who doesn't speak much English and is much more comfortable speaking Spanish, on one of their visits to the Chevy dealership. The salesman, who spoke Spanish, immediately began talking to the mom about the Chevy SUV's features and benefits. He also insisted that they take another test-drive (even though they had already done this), just so "Mom" could see how spacious and comfortable the vehicle was. During the test-drive, the salesman directed many of his comments and conversation to Mom. He asked about her background, her job, and her children and shared his own background and family stories. In a nutshell, he forged a bond.

A few days later, I asked this employee which SUV they were leaning toward. She replied, "It's so hard. The Toyota had more of the features we want and we like the color better, but the Chevy salesperson was *so nice* to my mom. I feel like I should do business with him."

I replied, "Really? You'd actually *not* buy the vehicle that better meets your needs because the salesman was nice to your mom? She's not even going to own or drive the vehicle!"

But that didn't matter to her. What made the greatest impression was the *treatment her mother received* from an attentive salesperson.

This type of story or anecdote is common among businesses that have Hispanic customers and that do a good job with creating a great experience for them. Pay attention to *abuelita* (grandma), and you may win the sale. Provide the kids with a toy, balloon, or coloring book, and you'll win the parents' hearts—and their wallets. Family is the center of many Hispanic customers' lives. If you take care of the whole family, you will create a deep and lasting relationship.

GOOD SERVICE CAN SAVE A BAD EXPERIENCE

Despite your best efforts and your best employees, sometimes mistakes are made. Employees, even good ones, screw up. But you can overcome those mistakes by providing Hispanic customers with killer customer service.

Have you ever shopped at a store that offered the opportunity to take a customer satisfaction survey on the bottom of your sales receipt? They usually provide a small offer or benefit for completing the survey. One of the largest companies that conducts these surveys (both online and on the phone) is based in Kansas City, Missouri. We did some work with them to determine whether there was a measurable difference in customer satisfaction between Hispanic and non-Hispanic consumers. They used two major national companies to conduct the test; one of the companies was a shoe retailer, and the other was a fast-food chain. They gathered data for six straight months to make sure they had a statistically viable sample size. The results were astonishing.

They found that if Hispanic customers felt they received "great customer service," which was defined by such simple, *and no-cost*, elements as a friendly smile, a warm greeting, making eye contact, and giving customers all the time they needed to make up their minds or make the purchase, they were apt to "forgive" other service *failures!* In other words, if you were warm and kind to Hispanic customers but forgot the fries or the chicken sandwich was cold, that was okay. The Hispanic customers still gave high customer satisfaction scores, even though their order was screwed up. The non-Hispanic customers behaved very differently: no matter how warm and kind you are, if you screw up the order, you're toast. The non-Hispanic customers didn't just score the stores lower for making a mistake; they *slammed* them.

This is a culturally profound insight—and a profound business opportunity. No business is perfect; we all make mistakes. But isn't it nice to know that *if you provide the one thing you can always control—an inviting environment* through warmth, sincerity, friendliness, patience, and kindness—your customer will forgive your mistakes and stay with you? Clearly, you want to run the best business you can and make as few errors as possible. But since you inevitably *will* make errors from time to time, it should comfort you to know that when you do, your Hispanic customers will not abandon you or think less of you, as long as the overall experience was pleasant, warm, and friendly.

I found this to be a very encouraging finding, and you should, too.

CHAPTER 12
Serving Different Racial and Ethnic Communities

Study after study has shown that marketing to specific racial and ethnic communities pays big dividends. Every customer wants to feel recognized, valued, and welcomed, and one way to effectively communicate all of that is to market to a specific group. When your marketing addresses a specific customer segment, you validate that group's importance to your business. You send a clear message that tells them, "We want to earn your business, so please consider our product/service when you are making your purchase decision."

Studies have also shown that not only do different racial and ethnic groups respond enthusiastically to the companies and brands that specifically market to them but they also become *loyal, repeat* customers. And that means sales growth and profitability for your business.

For most of this book, I have deliberately stayed away from the subject of marketing to specific groups because marketing is such a deep topic. It's broad and expansive, and there are numerous ways to do it right—and wrong. I also covered marketing to specific, diverse customer segments in my book *How to Market to People Not Like You: "Know It or Blow It" Rules for Reaching Diverse Customers.*

But I think it's appropriate to touch on marketing to different racial and ethnic groups in this section. Far too often, brands overlook a specific group's potential and instead lump everyone into one general marketing campaign. That approach doesn't do anything to make someone feel singled out as a valued customer. You can start growing your business with people not like you by using your marketing efforts to put the welcome mat out.

Marketing and customer service are two sides of the same coin. Marketing is what will bring new potential customers to your door. But what will make them buy—and then *buy again and again*—is the customer experience they have with you. And if that is a warm, welcoming, positive one, you can not only retain those customers as loyal, repeat buyers but also count on them to tell their friends, family, and social networks about their satisfaction.

Referrals are the best form of marketing there is. They cost you nothing and work harder for you than any ad campaign ever will, because people *trust* their friends and family. Think about it: your loved ones typically don't stand to gain anything by referring you to—or away from—a business. They make referrals because *they care about you* and want to see you well taken care of. By providing you with information about a business, product, or service, they are guiding you to what they feel is best for you. This is a selfless act of kindness and love. It's about *you*. That's why we trust the referrals and recommendations we get from people we love and respect. And that's why referrals are so powerful.

In Chapter 3, I covered the purchase funnel, the process we all undergo when we decide to buy something. You may recall that the first stage of the funnel is awareness. That's where marketing comes in. Marketing makes you aware that a company, business, product, or service exists and introduces you to the benefits and features of that product or service. Marketing is where the customer experience begins.

Marketing is where the customer experience *begins.*

Marketing doesn't only mean advertising. It can include that, but it can also include things such as distribution and availability of your product or service, sampling, promotional efforts, public relations efforts, community outreach and involvement, staffing and hiring, and even your hours of operation. Every customer touch point can be considered part of marketing, because such touch points all work to paint a picture of your product or service. And all communicate something to your customers and prospects. What you want that to be, of course, is that you value your prospective customers; you have a quality product or service that you're sure they need, and you want to earn their business. If you don't complete the marketing step correctly, how can you expect to move your prospective customers to the next stage of the purchase funnel? How can they ever become loyal, enthusiastic advocates of yours? It starts with marketing.

BLACKS AND AFRICAN AMERICANS

First, let's be clear about what I mean when I say that you should market to a specific group. There is no single specific "African American consumer profile," just as there is no "white," "Asian," or "Hispanic" profile. We are all different and most of the categories that marketers develop to define us do a pretty superficial job of it. However, here are *some* generalities and overarching insights and consumer comments that I believe will help you in crafting a customer experience that will reach and appeal to your African American prospects and customers.

Insight #1: *Show* People of Color When *Targeting* People of Color

One of the most powerful insights that I've heard was a comment someone made in an African American focus group. The group was composed of African American men and women of different ages, of different backgrounds, and from different cities. The discussion topic was how African Americans were portrayed in advertising and how the group felt about marketing to blacks. One woman in the group, Kim Edwards, a successful business owner, stated that she was drawn to almost any ad where she could "fit in." I asked her what she meant by that, and she explained: "As blacks, we haven't been [portrayed] in ads for very long. It's only recently that we've started seeing images of people who look like us in ads. We've been absent from marketing efforts for so long, that we're trained to 'get in where we fit in' ... If I see an ad for a product, and there's no person in the ad, I can picture that product being for me. I can see myself using [it]. Or if there's a person who's brown or black, I can 'fit myself into that ad.' But if [the] person in the ad is white, then I don't feel as much of a connection, because I don't look like that." When Edwards made this comment, the entire focus group came alive and nodded their agreement. Others in the group shared similar feelings: "We've been overlooked for so long. We immediately identify when we see a person of color in an ad, because for the longest time, we haven't been in many ads."

This is such a simple truth that it's hard to believe it's an insight; the fact is that we humans always relate to others just like us. That's why ads for retirement and financial planning always feature people in their 50s and 60s, because retirement is very much on the minds of people those ages. Your potential customers will more readily identify this as "an ad or product that's relevant to me" if they see someone in the ad who looks like they're facing the same concerns or desires that they are. So it's no surprise that most African Americans will take note of ads or marketing efforts that feature African Americans. In fact, a study by research firm Yankelovich, Inc. shows that 70 percent of African Americans say it's very important to them to see African Americans in ads.

Insight #2: Diversity in Skin Tone Is Very Important

You may have noticed that I use the terms *black* and *people of color*, as well as *African American*. This is because all over the world, diversity in skin color is no longer confined to shades of white, black, or brown. There is a range of skin color, from very light to very dark, and everything in between. In addition, as societies have become more mobile and integrated, it's not uncommon for people to be of mixed races. Those who are biracial or multiracial often identify themselves as a *person of color* rather than *black* or *white*, since this term more aptly captures a much broader definition of color than does *black* or *white*. In fact, a young woman in an African American focus group stated that she liked a particular ad for sneakers just because it featured a young girl who she said "looks like my sister." The young woman stated, "I have one black parent and one white parent, so my sister and I are mixed and we're very light-skinned African Americans. With freckles! But the girl in this ad looks just like my sister, with brown wavy hair and freckles and a light brown complexion. And she has a smile just like my sister, so it immediately caught my eye." Another woman in the same focus group added,

"Most of us have people in our families or social circles who are very light skinned or very black and every color in between. So if you show any range of brown or black, we can relate." The message is clear: make an effort to show diversity in skin tone if you feature people of color in your marketing efforts.

Insight #3: Food, Music, and Socializing Are Central to African American Culture

It seems that every culture revolves around food and music—and African American culture is no different. Socializing with friends and family is an important part of African American life, so presenting opportunities that weave these together can really boost the customer experience. One of the most insightful examples of using socializing to enrich the customer experience for African Americans is the Black Barbershop Health Outreach Program.

The barbershop experience is a highly social one for black men. Daniel Eaton, an executive at top U.S. marketing firm Epsilon, explains: "As black men, we go to our neighborhood barbershop and it's an experience like no other. Black men will spend hours at the barbershop, discussing everything from politics to current events and news, to our families and jobs. It's a unique bonding experience [at] a place we trust. We can be ourselves, talk openly, joke around, and spend time with our buddies."

Given the special place that the barbershop is for black men, as well as the fact that black men suffer worse health than any other racial or ethnic group in the United States, it makes perfect sense to use barbershops as a safe and trusted place to disseminate important health information. The goal of the Black Barbershop Health Outreach Program, instituted in 38 U.S. cities, is to increase awareness and education about key health issues for black men. Sounds like a great community service, right? It is. But think about the *hundreds of black barbershops that participate in the program* and how much it enhances and enriches the total customer experience for barbershop patrons. Here is a safe and trusted place where men gather to get haircuts and perhaps shaves. And while there, they learn about specific health risks or issues that affect black men—and get resource information as well. Wouldn't you naturally think that the barbershop respects and values black men? After all, what can possibly be a greater sign of respect than caring about your health and well-being? Simply by participating in the Black Barbershop Health Outreach Program, barbershops are clearly communicating that they value their black customers.

Another example of tapping into the importance of socializing is what Magic Johnson did with his theaters (located in New York and Maryland) and his Starbucks locations in the Detroit area. Magic Johnson was convinced that although African Americans enjoy the same movies as whites, they would enjoy watching them more amid an audience of their own because they could shout with impunity. "We like yelling at that screen," he explained. The Magic Theater refreshments have been "tweaked toward minorities," Magic says, with sweeter drinks and spicy sausage. In his Starbucks, you could buy sweet potato pie and also hear a wider variety of music than in other Starbucks, including Stevie Wonder and Miles Davis. By tweaking the basic product or service (movies or coffee shop environment), Magic successfully demonstrated that he *values, respects, and wants* African American customers.

Insight #4: Make No Assumptions

Despite the fact that this part is so simple, *so many* businesses get it all wrong. Simply treat African Americans and people of color with the same respect and courtesy *that you treat anyone else*. It's not about trying to connect with them on a racial or ethnic basis. Blacks and African Americans want to buy your product or service because it will help their lives or provide a solution for them in some way. Greet every customer with sincerity, warmth, and respect and make no assumptions. About what, you ask? Well, income and ability to afford certain products or services, for one thing. According to Chandra Livingston, a vice president and independent consultant for a global beauty, health, and wellness company, "So often when I go into a luxury store, the clerk assumes that I can't afford the items in the store and often will not even ask, 'May I help you?' Like other communities, there are affluent African Americans who enjoy high-end goods and services. The store clerks who show respect to me when I come through the door—just like they do with everyone else—will earn my buying loyalty."

An even worse, and incredibly offensive, assumption is that your customers of color will somehow rip you off. As Kim Edwards stated, "The most insulting thing you can do to me as a potential customer in your store is to follow me around." I expressed shock when she said this, and she replied, "Sadly, it happens all the time. I guess retailers think I'm going to steal from them." *Wow.* Talk about a situation in which your employees *destroy* the customer experience! Make no assumptions about customers of color other than that they are sincerely interested in what your product or service can do for them.

Here are some dos and don'ts for crafting a great customer experience for people of color:

Do

- Do be **honest,** straightforward, and consistent in your pricing and business practices.
- Do be **dependable.** Show respect for others' time and make sure your product or service is doing what you've promised.
- Do **ask for referrals** from your happy and satisfied customers.
- Do **be sincere** in your efforts. Don't just try to make money off the African American consumer. Cultivate an ongoing, loyal relationship between the customer and your business, and the money will follow.
- Do **get involved in and support the African American community.**
- Do **connect with the community where they are:** neighborhoods, salons, barbershops, churches, restaurants, and clubs.

Don't

- Don't **be pushy** and try to oversell. Explain your product or service, tout its features and benefits, and then let the consumer make an informed decision.
- Don't **try to be too cool** or hip. Just be who you are.

- "Don't try to connect with me by **telling me you've got a black friend.**" This comment was echoed in many consumer focus groups: "I don't care if you've got a black friend. Just connect with me by being a good business with a product or service I need at fair prices."
- Don't **make assumptions about financial status.** "It's so insulting when someone assumes that I have weak credit or don't care about the stock market just because I'm black. I make good money, I have investments, and I take care of my finances just like anyone else." Although this insight and comment came from a focus group with African American consumers, I think it applies to any customer segment, regardless of age, ethnicity, gender, or language spoken. It's never okay to assume that an entire customer group isn't financially capable of buying your product or service.
- Don't **try to connect on a superficial level.** An African American woman tells of a salesperson at an appliance store who tried to make small talk with her by asking her if she liked Beyoncé and Jay-Z's music. "It felt so weird and superficial to me to have this salesman chat with me about music because I know he was doing it just because I'm black. I would have much rather discussed the features of the washing machine I was looking to buy."

People of color can be your best customers. They want to know about your products and services. They want your recognition, your respect, and your marketing efforts. Use these insights to craft a customer experience that delivers validation and satisfaction and watch your sales and profits grow.

Insight #5: Get Involved with and Support the Community

As in Chapter 11 on Hispanic consumers, I recommend that you get involved in the African American community's needs and find a way to contribute if you want to target this group. Whether it's through educational, family, or health efforts; faith organizations; or expansion of community resources, you can successfully market to people of color by showing that you're committed to their community. It's important that the target consumers of all diversity marketing feel recognized and valued for *who they are*, not just the size of their wallets. You don't just want to sell someone your product or service today; you want to keep them as a customer for life. And becoming involved in the community is a tangible way to show your support and ongoing appreciation of a consumer group.

Your efforts to become involved don't have to be large or expensive. It's easy to start locally. Look around and ask people to find out what's needed. Perhaps you could sponsor a local children's sports team that needs jerseys. Perhaps a playground needs some repairs, or a school needs a few new computers. Maybe having a booth at a local health fair or festival is a way to spread word of your company, product, or service while helping support the event. Becoming involved in the African American community will give you insights into what your potential customers want and how you can best provide it to them.

Although people of color live all over the world, this chapter is focused on how to market to people of color in the United States. Why? Because the United States tends to have more of a racial divide than European countries, Canada, and other places in the world. Although race relations continue to improve in the United States, there still exists a "difference" in the U.S. African American consumer market compared with what is commonly called the general market (non–African American). Your company or brand can make a big difference in this area by taking small steps that not only enhance the customer's experience but also position you as a supporter of diverse communities and customers. Your "welcome mat" matters. And putting the welcome mat out for people of color will grow your business, today and tomorrow.

ASIANS AND ASIAN AMERICANS

From a marketing perspective, the strength of the Asian population is pretty irrefutable. It's the largest population in the world, numbering nearly 8 billion as of this writing. In the United States and Canada, Asian Americans have the highest household income of any race or ethnicity. So whether you're trying to sell shoes in China or home mortgages in Canada, learning about the Asian market is certainly worth your time.

So what is the definition of *Asian?* It varies from country to country, but the most common definition is a person who descends from East Asia, South Asia, or Southeast Asia. Here are some (but not all) of the groups that are considered Asian:

Chinese	Palestinian
Indian	Laotian
Filipino	Taiwanese
Pakistani	Indonesian
Korean	Malaysian
Vietnamese	Thai
Lebanese	Jordanian
Iranian	Burmese
Sri Lankan	Tibetan
Japanese	Sakha
Afghani	Mongolian
Syrian	Nepali
Iraqi	Saudi
Cambodian	Yemeni
Bangladeshi	Singaporean

The U.S. Asian Population

Current estimates indicate that about 5 percent of the U.S. population reports themselves as having either full or partial Asian heritage (approximately 15 million people). The largest ethnic subgroups are Chinese, Filipinos, Indians, Vietnamese, Koreans, and Japanese. Other sizable groups are Cambodian/Khmer, Pakistanis, Laotians, Hmong, and Thais.

Geographically, the top places in the United States for marketing to Asians are California and New York, because there are large concentrations of the Asian population, combined with high income and buying power, as well as many Asian media outlets. In addition, Asian youth tend to fit a profile of exactly what marketers hunger for:

tech-savvy, early adopters who value style and function and who watch trends carefully. They're also very connected to friends and family, both online and offline.

Following are some key steps to marketing to Asian consumers in a relevant manner, which is the beginning of the customer experience with your business.

Step 1: Evaluate the "Size of the Prize"

If your product or service is sold in an area with a large Asian population, you don't want to miss out on the opportunity to reach this market. For example, one in five people in San Francisco are Asian. If you market in this region, you'd absolutely want to make this consumer group aware of your product or service.

Do your homework and determine whether the size of the Asian population in a given area merits developing an Asian marketing plan. And don't just review population numbers; look at the *percentage of the population* as well. For example, you might not think of Millbourne, Pennsylvania, as a place that would have a major Asian market. And although the town's population is only 943 people, 54 percent of them are Asian. So if I had a small business in a place where more than half the residents are Asian, I'd certainly value the size of the prize and make every effort to reach the local Asian community in a meaningful way.

Step 2: Learn about Which Subsegment Represents Your Greatest Market Opportunity

Because there are so many different Asian subsegments—all of which have different languages, holidays, cultures, and traditions—it's crucial to understand your target consumer group as much as possible. Are they Chinese? Vietnamese? Korean? You can find this information easily on sites like Wikipedia, Freedemographics.com, or Census.gov. You can drill down to even small towns and places and learn about the local Asian population. Since different cultures have different holidays, many local marketing opportunities, such as festivals and fairs, will vary based on which population you're serving.

Step 3: Explore Asian Media Options

Once you've determined that there is a viable market opportunity with Asian consumers, educate yourself about local Asian media options. In Dallas, for example, there is a large Vietnamese population and a weekly newspaper called *But Viet* that serves the Vietnamese community. This paper enjoys a strong, stable weekly readership, not only because it is in Vietnamese, but because it covers news and information from Vietnam that are of interest to its readers. And since it's a small newspaper, advertising is relatively inexpensive and advertisers get results when they advertise in it.

Step 4: Make Sure You Use Qualified Translation Services, If Necessary

It is essential to make sure that any marketing message you craft in another language has an accurate, appropriate, and meaningful translation. This is especially important if you don't read Asian language characters. Unlike many languages with alphabets, written Asian languages use characters. Therefore, unless you know how to read the characters, you're not going to be able to proofread your message. You will need to rely upon a translation service or media outlet to do this for you. Most Asian media offer this service free of charge. They know that companies and brands that typically advertise in English aren't equipped to develop a message in an Asian language, so they provide this service at no charge. Take advantage of it, and let the media outlet do the work on this for you.

But what if you're not using a media outlet such as a newspaper or radio station? Suppose those options are simply too cost-prohibitive, and you just want to create some flyers that are targeted to Asians in your community. What then? In this case, develop your message in your primary language (for example, English) and then hire a *certified* translation company to adapt or transcreate the message. It's very important that you use a translation service that certifies their work, because they're essentially guaranteeing that your message will be error free. Although mistakes can, of course, happen any time, with any company, a certified translation service will stand behind their work and make restitution if there is a problem that arises from the translation they provided. You can imagine how important certified translations are to certain businesses: anything legal, technical, or financial needs to be precise and 100 percent accurate. There is no room for "interpretation" of an insurance policy application, for example. You may pay a little more to use a certified translation service, but it's well worth the peace of mind you'll enjoy.

IMMIGRANTS AND RECENT ARRIVALS

Why do people move from one country to another? The top two reasons are (1) economic opportunity, the pursuit of a better life, and (2) family reunification. People all around the globe leave their home countries behind to follow their dreams and build better lives for themselves and their loved ones.

Whether they stay for a few months, for a few years, or for the rest of their lives, immigrants are an important part of every country's economy. New arrivals to a country buy goods and services. And if you treat immigrants as welcome customers to your business, most of the time you will be rewarded with loyal customers who will bring you even more business through referrals. Imagine yourself moving to a foreign country and really not knowing your way around, where to shop, where to do business—not even being aware of basic things like where to get your hair cut or do your grocery shopping. What would you do? How would you begin to figure it all out?

One of the first things you might do is find out where the communities of your fellow compatriots live. In almost every city and country, there are communities of immigrants who live in close proximity to one another. When you think about it, it's quite logical: as you adapt to a new home, you'd initially want to live around others like yourself—people who speak your language and understand your native culture. These people would be able to show you the ropes and help you adjust to your new life in this new city or country, because they'd immigrated there before you and have experience with the process. They would be able to advise you on what to do or not do. They could point you to the grocery stores that carry your country's or region's ethnic foods so that you could cook meals you like and are familiar with. They'd be able to direct you to businesses and people whom they found to be helpful and with whom they feel comfortable. And they would tell you to avoid places where someone had been rude to them, overcharged them, or didn't provide good service or even simply someplace where they'd felt unwelcome.

As a new arrival to a new city, area, or country, you'd probably follow their recommendations closely. It would save you a lot of time and hassle. You wouldn't have to figure everything out on your own; you'd let others who had experienced it all before guide you. This is why, all across the world, humans gravitate toward others like themselves, particularly when they find themselves in a new and unfamiliar place.

So how does this phenomenon affect you and your business? If your business is located in a place where there is a large or growing immigrant population, you can prosper greatly by serving these customers. Your business can grow immediately by making sales to immigrants, and if they are happy and satisfied with your product or service, they will almost certainly refer you to others who will do more business with you. This can be an enormously effective way to grow your business, because as you know, referrals cost you nothing. You don't have to spend money on advertising or marketing; you simply need to do a great job taking care of each and every customer. Attracting immigrant groups to your business is a smart strategy, but it's important that you know that not all immigrants are the same. There is a process that each immigrant goes through called acculturation, and because it is a process, not all people will be in the same phase at the same time. In other words, immigrants are not one size fits all. Let me explain.

ACCULTURATION, NOT ASSIMILATION

Every immigrant who arrives in a new country goes through the process of acculturation. It doesn't matter if you are Polish and move to Switzerland, are an American who moves to Greece, or are British and move to India. Regardless of who you are and where you're from, you will experience acculturation if you move to another country.

And although many people use the word *acculturation* interchangeably with *assimilation*, they really shouldn't. The two words actually have very different meanings. *Assimilation* means you forfeit your culture and adopt the habits and traditions of a new culture. *Acculturation* means that you retain aspects of your primary culture that you value while also adopting aspects of a new culture. With acculturation, there are certain things you like and want from a new culture; however, there are certain things that you want to maintain from your primary culture, too. Think of it this way: assimilation is about "either/or" (for example, I'm either Hungarian or I'm British), whereas acculturation is about "and" (for example, I'm Hungarian and I'm also British).

Acculturation is the merging of two cultures in close contact. It's what happens when a person moves to a new country or is exposed to a country's culture, values, and lifestyles.

And because it is a *process*, people move through it in varying degrees and at varying speeds. Some people acculturate very rapidly to a new culture; others never really acculturate much at all.

There are four distinct mind-sets that reflect the differing levels of acculturation among immigrants:

1. **Cultural loyalist:** This refers to a foreign-born, recent arrival who has typically been in the new country for less than 5 years, and certainly less than 10. Because it takes a long time to learn a new language, this person depends on his or her native language to communicate and likely consumes mostly native-language media and marketing messages. This individual will often live and work among other immigrants from his or her homeland and tends to hold onto the native country's traditional values. Although cultural loyalists may spend the rest of their lives living in their new, adopted country, many dream of going back "home." In focus groups with cultural loyalists, we'll often hear comments like, "I am here working, trying to save up enough money to buy a little house back home." This is why these individuals are called cultural loyalists; although they live in one country, their heart and their dreams are "back home." They are loyal to their primary culture. They do not consider their adopted home to be their true home, but rather, a place to live and work for the time being.

2. **Cultural embracer:** This person is also foreign-born but has chosen to make the new country his or her *permanent* home. Cultural embracers left their country of origin knowing that they are *not* going back. They may have immigrated for educational, professional, or occupational opportunities; because they are married to or in love with a citizen of another country; or for some other reason. Because they have adopted another country as their new home, they do not have a visitor mentality. They eagerly embrace new foods, music, and traditions and seek to make new friends. That's why they are called *embracers;* they welcome everything about their new, adopted home. People in this group tend to be slightly more educated and have very aspirational goals. Although they may be bilingual or multilingual, they prefer their native tongue. How could they not? As foreign-born individuals, their native tongue will always be their first language, and consequently, the easiest way for them to express themselves.
3. **Cross-culturer:** People in this group are the first generation to be born in the adopted country. Their parents are foreign-born. Cross-culturers are bilingual, typically having learned the family's native language first at home and the new country's language at school. Because Mom and Dad (and often Grandma and Grandpa) are all foreign-born, the family communicates primarily in the native language and holds dear many traditions from their original country. The result is that cross-culturers are not only bilingual but also *bicultural*—equally comfortable with both the old and new countries' cultures. They also live and work in two languages with ease.

   Cross-culturers may be verbally fluent in the language of their parents' country. However, this does not mean that they know how to read and write that language well. This is because their education and focus in school was on learning to read and write in the language of the country in which they were born and currently live. Therefore, although they may be able to converse in their family's native tongue, it doesn't necessarily mean that they know the proper grammar or punctuation, the rules of accents, and so on. This is important to note, because we often have clients with someone on their staff who falls into this acculturation category. Because this person *speaks* another language, the client expects that individual to help write or translate a brochure into that language. However, the person's formal education and training in reading and writing often doesn't qualify him or her to do this. Cross-culturers see themselves as members of both cultures: that of their family's background and that of the country in which they were born. They are very much in touch with their roots and their heritage.

4. **Cultural integrator:** Individuals in this group are fully acculturated. Although they were born in one country, they trace their roots and ancestry to another country. This person may not speak the language of his or her ancestry well or at all. Cultural integrators are usually more dependent on the language of the country in which they were born. However, they tend to be very proud of their foreign heritage, and consequently, they experience a form of retro-acculturation. Because these individuals are already fully acculturated, their acculturation process has them returning to their roots and embracing their history and traditions. That's retro-acculturation—the effort of reclaiming or getting back in touch with your cultural roots.

Figure 12.1 summarizes the four levels of acculturation.

As you can imagine, a cultural loyalist's customer experience and needs will differ greatly from those of a cultural integrator. Let's take banking as an example. Suppose you're the marketing director of a bank for a community that has a sizable and growing Indian population. You know that this represents opportunity for your bank, so you want to create relevant marketing messages to entice potential Indian customers to your bank.

The first thing to do would be to identify the right products for the right Indian profile. For example, the cultural loyalist is a recent arrival, so chances are that he or she will need basic financial services, such as a savings and checking account. This customer may also need and want money wiring services, since it's very likely that he or she is sending money each week to a loved one "back home." This person may also require some financial literacy and education, since

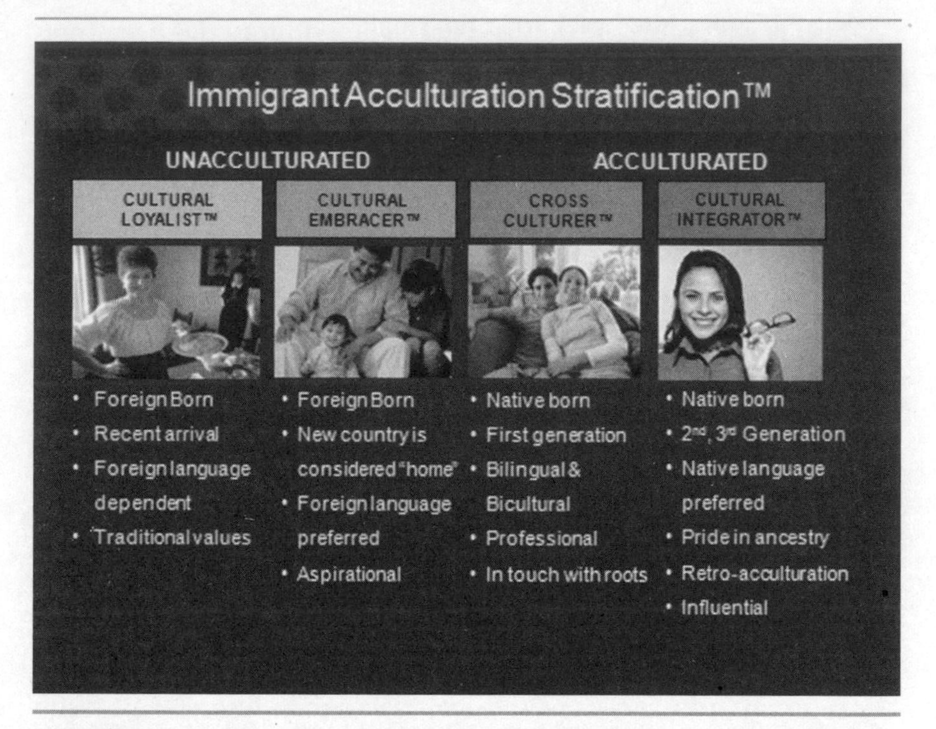

FIGURE 12.1 The acculturation model summarizes the stages of acculturation that immigrants go through.

many people who come from India have little or no experience with using financial institutions. It would *not* be practical, of course, to try to market mortgage products to this individual. A recently arrived person isn't likely to have yet built up the credit history necessary to get approved for a mortgage.

You could market your checking, savings, and money wiring services and perhaps market auto loans or mobile banking to the cultural embracer. And there's probably no need to market money wiring services to the cross-culturer at all, since that person's parents are here in the new country as well. However, *this* consumer makes an excellent mortgage and perhaps even small business loan prospect. And the cultural integrator can take advantage of all the bank's products and services, with the exception perhaps of money wiring.

This example showcases how you might approach the immigrant customer based on acculturation. However, to craft an exceptional customer experience for immigrants and new arrivals, you'll want to educate yourself about their customs and traditions. This will allow you to create the most welcoming environment possible. And to do that, it's important to understand that some of the customs we take for granted every day can be not only strange to others but actually offensive.

For example, Americans tend to assume that everyone wants to be greeted with a firm handshake. It never crosses our minds that many people, especially new immigrants, don't want to have their hands shaken. In fact, it can be extremely uncomfortable for them. For instance, it can be very offensive for anyone who isn't her husband to touch an older female customer from India or a traditional Japanese or Middle Eastern country. Many other cultures are very uncomfortable with shaking hands, simply because they aren't familiar with the custom. Most Americans assume that shaking hands is standard business practice across the globe when, in fact, it's not. The most popular form of greeting around the world is the bow. Although there are too many cultures and traditions to review here—and each is different in its own way—there are some general guidelines to follow that will serve you well for any customer group.

Here are some tips for providing good customer service to immigrants and recent arrivals:

1. **Smile and warmly welcome everyone to your business.** Friendliness is universal, and everyone understands a smile, as it's the ultimate "welcome mat."
2. **Do your homework and learn the customs, traits, and traditions of your immigrant customers.** Apply what you've learned in your business. For example, Hispanic culture is more social than U.S. culture in business. A business e-mail in the United States is typically short and very much to the point. Yet that same directness would be considered rude in Latin America. Business correspondence is more personal in these cultures; therefore, it is not uncommon for colleagues to ask about how your family is and

how your vacation was, *then* move onto the business reason for the correspondence.

3. **Don't assume that everyone knows how to use everyday items.** Some everyday items, such as electronics, may not be so commonplace in other parts of the world. Ask customers if they would like you to demonstrate your product for them.
4. **Show patience.** Many immigrants and recent arrivals have lots of questions when making a purchase or doing research to determine whether your offering is truly what they need. They may have more questions than you typically encounter. Be patient and give them all the time that they need to digest information and make a decision.
5. **Don't ever misrepresent your product or service or exploit your prospective customers' naiveté.** People from other countries may initially be unfamiliar with products or services that you offer, but they will learn quickly if they have been told the truth in a purchase transaction. And people can handle the truth. It's better to tell your prospective customers the strengths and limitations of what you're selling ("We do have this item on sale, but because it is a clearance item, it is not returnable once you buy it") than to overpromise or neglect to mention an important aspect.
6. **Remember that talking louder does not make someone bilingual.** It's astonishing how many times I've seen this: a clerk at a store is trying to help someone who doesn't speak English, and the clerk keeps raising his or her voice until he or she is practically shouting at the customer. That doesn't create effective communication; it simply creates noise and makes the customer uneasy.
7. **Train your staff on cultural sensitivity.** Teach your sales force that cultural differences among customers and prospects are not wrong, just different. For example, MetroPCS is a telecommunications provider with a large network of independent owners and operators. A significant percentage of their dealer base is Korean. They devote an entire section of their Standard Operating Procedures manual at the corporate headquarters to Korean culture. All new employees are expected to read the manual and demonstrate respect for the cultural values of their "customers" (their dealers).

Being sensitive to the needs of immigrants and recent arrivals simply says, "We care." And when you show people you care, they will come back to you over and over again. If you take the time to learn the unique needs of customers who are new to your country or community, it will improve your bottom line. These customers will buy from you and tell their entire network of friends and family to buy from you as well.

CHAPTER 13
Gay, Lesbian, Bisexual, and Transgendered Customers

Two of my friends bought a house together not long ago. It was their first house, and they were really excited about it. Buying your first house is a thrilling—and terrifying—experience, since there's a lot to know about this big step. So they were both understandably a little stressed out about it. They're very meticulous, organized people who did their homework on all the ins and outs of buying a home.

However, they were disappointed when shopping for mortgages to find that instead of making things easier for them, the mortgage brokers actually *added* to the stress of the situation. They found that aspect of the process to be very difficult in meeting after meeting with various brokers and lenders. Why? Because my friends Dave and Don are gay. Their very presence, sitting in a bank across from a loan officer or across the desk from a broker, made these loan executives uncomfortable. As Dave stated to me, "You could tell these guys had no experience with a gay couple trying to get a mortgage. They were so nervous—couldn't even look [either one of] us in the eye! Why would I want to do business with someone who can't even look me in the eye?"

So Dave and Don ended up using a mortgage broker from the Gay Mortgage Directory.

Although I am glad they had a resource like the Gay Mortgage Directory to help them find a broker, it shouldn't have come to that. A same-sex couple *should* be able to sit across from a loan officer at a bank or credit union and be able to transact business without being made to feel uncomfortable. And let's face it, this is *business*. I recognize that there are people whose values or faith disapprove of same-sex relationships, but you can't let your personal feelings dictate how you handle a customer. Customers have the right to have businesses treat them with respect and fairness across the board. Even if you wouldn't be comfortable *socializing* with same-sex couples, you must be able to serve their business needs and craft a favorable customer experience. Business isn't about dealing with the world on your terms. It's about dealing with the world *the way the world is*. And that requires that you maximize each and every opportunity for sales growth and customer retention.

The gay, lesbian, bisexual, and transgender market (hereafter referred to as GLBT) is lucrative and very loyal. Large companies and major global brands figured out decades ago that it pays dividends to put the welcome mat out for GLBT consumers. It's an affluent and educated market consisting of very loyal consumers. Of gays and lesbians, 89 percent say they are highly likely to seek out brands that advertise specifically to them. And even if you don't market or advertise specifically to the GLBT market, they will reward you with repeat business and referrals if you provide a great customer experience for them. And isn't that what we, as businesspeople, all want: happy, satisfied customers who keep coming back, doing more business with us, and who become advocates referring others to us?

As with so many customer segments, the GLBT market is a tight-knit community in most places. Many gays and lesbians know and socialize with other gay friends. Consequently, there is tremendous opportunity for networking and sharing of information—good *and* bad—about customer experiences and business recommendations.

The travel and tourism industry recognized long ago that the GLBT market represented huge business potential. But there are literally thousands of websites, chat rooms, and blog posts about GLBT travelers having horrible vacation experiences, all because of poor customer service. In other words, the horror stories aren't about a dirty hotel room or lackluster food. These complaints are about *people on staff treating them poorly or embarrassing them*. Here's an example from one of my gay friend's last vacation experience. He and his boyfriend had done extensive research on where to go on vacation and which hotel to stay at—and they chose carefully. They picked a centrally located hotel that was close to all the activities and things they wanted to see and do. It was perfect; it had all the features and amenities they wanted at the right price. They booked a room with a king-size bed and looked forward to their trip for weeks.

When they checked in, the young man at the front desk pulled up their reservation and said, "Oh, they booked you in a room with a king bed. I'll switch that to two queen beds for you." My friend and his boyfriend looked at each other, then said to the front desk clerk, "No, we booked a king. We'll take a king. That's what we want."

At that point, the front desk clerk said, "You want to sleep together in the same bed?" Then, as it dawned on him that my friend and his boyfriend are a couple, the clerk blurted out, "Oh! You're *gay!*" He said this loudly, and others in the hotel lobby turned to stare. My friend and his boyfriend were mortified. Something as simple as checking into a hotel and getting the room you've reserved without commentary or embarrassment from a hotel associate should be fundamental to providing a great customer experience—*for anyone*. Gay or straight, old or young, black or white, checking into a hotel with your partner should not be an awkward or embarrassing experience. And if it starts like that at the front desk, how can that not taint the entire experience?

GayComfort is a company that specializes in training companies and employees in the travel and hospitality industry on how to provide superior customer service to gay and lesbian travelers. According to GayComfort, *one in four gay consumers switched brands* last year to one they perceived to be more welcoming to them as a gay customer. And 7 in 10 stop using a brand *forever* if they receive bad service. GayComfort states that it's not about treating your lesbian and gay customers *differently* from other customers. It is about letting gay customers experience what most customers take for granted: *the ability to relax and be themselves.*

Perhaps there is no better definition of *vacation* than that: the ability to relax and be yourself. And how can you possibly do that if you are made to feel uncomfortable or someone is being rude, unkind, or just plain insensitive to you?

One of the best things you can do to effectively cultivate and show that you value the GLBT community is to "start at home" by ensuring that your business is gay-friendly. This means establishing nondiscrimination policies in the workplace, providing domestic partner or same-sex spousal insurance for employees, and offering other tangible benefits that show your place is also a good place to work. Many members of the gay community closely follow the workplace rankings provided by several GLBT organizations.

Second, remember that your employees can kill the customer experience for anyone. They need to show respect to your GLBT customers at all times. These individuals are not oddities, and it's definitely *not okay* to make personal comments about customers' sexuality or appearance. Following are some quotes from a focus group with gay and lesbian consumers. It's hard to believe that anyone would say such rude, insensitive, or downright inappropriate comments to a stranger—let alone a *potential customer*—but it happens:

- "Are you a lesbian? The reason I ask is because you have short hair."
- (To a transgendered woman): "Oh my gosh! Are you a man?! My uncle used to dress up in my aunt's clothes, too. He was such a freak."
- (From a waiter at a café to two men having lunch who were sharing bites of each other's meals): "Oh jeez, just cut it out, will you? You people make me sick."
- "Are you two together?" When the lesbian couple replied yes, the clerk said, "You're going to hell, you know."

It's hard to believe that people even think to utter such comments in this day and age, but they do. So make it ABSOLUTELY CLEAR to your staff that there is zero tolerance for rude, insensitive, prying, personal comments, and remarks such as these.

I want to address another issue that is important for your employees in crafting a great customer experience for your GLBT customers. Over the past few years, I have heard a number of young people use the word *gay* in a very derogatory way. Time and again, I hear young people say, "*That's so gay,*" when what they mean to express is that something is weird or stupid. It's a troubling expression, but a fairly common one. As an employer or manager, you need to let your team know that an expression like that is absolutely off-limits. It's a challenge to change the way people speak, since many people frequently adopt an expression and use it without thinking. If you have employees who say or may potentially use this phrase, your job is to let them know right away that using the word *gay* in that way is unacceptable and will not be tolerated. What if one of your customers overheard that? *And be aware that you don't have to be gay or lesbian to be highly offended by such an expression.*

Here are some other dos and don'ts for effectively cultivating the GLBT community, courtesy of the GLAAD (Gay & Lesbian Alliance

Against Defamation, www.glaad.org) Advertising Media Program Best Practices:

Dos

- Do **avoid using clichés** and alienating GLBT stereotypes and homophobia
- Do **become aware of the differences** between cross-dressers/transvestites, transsexuals, male-to-females, female-to-males, androgyny, and female impersonator/drag queens.
- Do recognize that GLBT people come from all races, ages, ethnicities, nationalities, incomes, political and religious affiliations, professions, physical abilities, and gender expressions, and whenever possible, incorporate such diversity into their representations. **One size does not fit all.**
- Do understand that **few consumers will shun your brand for being GLBT-friendly.**
- Do recognize that GLBT people **already are your customers.**
- Do understand it is important to **test GLBT-themed ads**, including those emphasizing masculine or feminine characteristics, with GLBT perspectives and in focus groups.

Don'ts

- Don't **engage social conservatives in debate regarding GLBT issues,** when criticized; business and respect for faith are separate issues.
- Don't **waffle, modify, or withdraw GLBT-friendly campaigns.** Be consistent and principled.
- Don't **hyperventilate about backlash and boycott threats.** Experience shows most provocation is politically motivated and intended for near-term shock and awe. Companies have found that these episodes almost always blow over quickly.
- Don't **use GLBT stereotypes,** themes, or people as a device to elicit shock, humor, or titillation.
- Don't **use horrified or violent revulsion** to references of homosexuality or transgender people.
- Don't **label or degrade** gay men or lesbians as sexual predators.

- Don't **use sexuality in a degrading way** to characterize same-sex affection and intimacy—or associate sexual practices with gays and lesbians differently from those of heterosexuals.
- Don't **characterize transgender people as deceptive**, scary, or freakish.
- Don't **characterize bisexuals as cheaters.**

GLBT customers are like any other customer group: they want good products and service, fair prices, and a great customer experience. Members of this group can represent a terrific growth opportunity for your business. It doesn't matter if you're gay or straight. What matters is that you sincerely recognize GLBT customers' business potential and take steps, internally and externally, to put the welcome mat out for this lucrative and loyal customer segment.

Conclusion

We've covered a lot of ground in this book. You've spent considerable time reading this, and I hope it's been helpful to you and given you some ideas to try in your own business. Or, at a minimum, I hope that it's inspired you to start thinking about ways you can craft an exceptional customer experience for different types of people. Going forward, this will be a key differentiator for your business as well as a powerful sales and customer retention strategy. Almost everything is in the hands of the consumer these days. From product information, to research on competitive companies and services, to information on pricing, to the ability to comparison shop and find less expensive alternatives elsewhere, to the level of community involvement your company has, customers can now know everything about you. And they base their decisions about whether to do business with you on some or all of these factors.

Other than being "the good guy"—being the company with stellar business ethics, fair and competitive pricing, progressive hiring practices and employee benefits, and a strong connection to your local community—there are many things you can't control. You can't control the economy. You can't control the stock market. You're probably not able to exert much control over the cost of goods and labor. But the one thing that is totally in your control at all times is the customer experience.

This should be an empowering thought. This should make you feel excited about serving your customers, because you can do so in ways that are meaningful to them. Your customers are already interested in what you sell or provide. They're 80 percent there. By giving them a customer experience that recognizes them, validates them, and delights them, you'll not only cement the other 20 percent but make serious deposits toward future business with them.

Your customers and your community are changing. Racially and ethnically, every community is more diverse today than ever before. But creating a customer experience for people not like you doesn't mean catering only to different racial and ethnic groups.

Moms are different from people who aren't moms. Gen Yers differ from baby boomers or matures. GLBT customers have different needs than those of straight customers. The physically challenged have different needs than those who are not. Men are different from women. People who live in large cities are different from people who live in small, rural areas.

Yet no matter how much different customer groups may not be like you, remember that they all want the same thing: a positive customer experience that makes them feel like you put the welcome mat out *just for them*.

When you do that, when you create a customer experience that satisfies your customer at every stage of the purchase funnel, you have moved beyond simply making a *transaction* with that customer. You have created a *relationship*. And that's a powerful place for you to be.

You are a smart, forward-thinking businessperson who is paying attention to the customer shifts around you. I applaud you for spending time reading this book to learn how to be an *even better* businessperson. It's clear that you respect your customers—and your prospects—because you've spent valuable time exploring ways to make doing business with you as good as it can be.

Take what you've learned here and apply it to your business. Follow the seven principles and stay attuned; keep paying attention to the shifts you see all around you. Keep being the smart businessperson that you are. You can craft an outstanding customer experience for anyone, even someone who is not like you. And when you do, you will see your sales, profits, and customer loyalty grow.

Index